Poems: Selected & New

POEMS:
Selected and New
1967 — 1991

Robert
Peters

SANTA MARIA
ASYLUM ARTS
1992

First appearances of some of these poems are acknowledged in the
author's Foreword.

ISBN 1-878589-30-2 (cloth)
ISBN 1-878580-31-0 (paper)

Library of Congress Catalogue Number: 92-71208

Cover illustration by Meredith Peters.

Asylum Arts
P. O. Box 6203
Santa Maria, CA 93456

Contents

III: GARY

FOREWORD

Poems: Selected and New 1967-1991 brings together the poems I most care to save from my earliest books: *Songs for A Son* (W. W. Norton, 1967); *The Sow's Head and Other Poems* (Wayne State University Press, 1968); *Bronchial Tangle, Heart System* (Granite Books, 1975); *Cool Zebras of Light* (Christopher's Books, 1975); *Gauguin's Chair: Selected Poems 1964-1974* (Crossing Press, 1977); *The Drowned Man to the Fish* (New Rivers, 1978); *What John Dillinger Meant to Me* (Sea Horse Press, 1983); *Brueghel's Pig* (Illuminati, 1989); *Good Night, Paul* (GLB Publishers, 1992). All of the above titles except for *The Drowned Man to the Fish* and *Good Night, Paul* are now out of print.

Some poems appear here in book form for the first time. I have also included a generous sampling from seven of my eight book-length voice or persona books: *The Gift to be Simple* (Liveright, 1975), *Ludwig of Bavaria* (New Rivers, 1982; Cherry Valley, 1986), *The Blood Countess* (Cherry Valley, 1987), *Hawker* (Unicorn, 1985), *Kane* (Unicorn, 1986), *Shaker Light* (Unicorn, 1988), and *Haydon* (Unicorn, 1989). Only the most recent of the persona books, *Snapshots for a Serial Killer* (GLB Publishers, 1992) is not represented. Also not fully represented are my books of satires, parodies, surrealist and collage poems: *Holy Cow: Parable Poems, The Poet As Ice-Skater,* and *Celebrities: In Memory of Margaret Dumont.*

Making choices has been difficult. First, the bulk of the work published over the two decades since *Songs for A Son* is formidable. Second, how can I be objective about which are worth preserving? Poets are notoriously inept self-critics. Third, how might I best create readability—by hewing to a strict chronological arrangement, or by themes? I have opted for the latter, although my choices remain broadly chronological.

Part One contains selections from my first book, the elegies on the death by meningitis of my 4 1/2 year old son Richard. This loss directed me towards writing poetry as a way of maintaining my sanity.

Part Two treats my northern Wisconsin boyhood and youth, and is largely from *What Dillinger Meant to Me.* The final poems, on the deaths of my parents, new, are included to round out the suite. Readers interested in my approach to this material in prose may wish to read *Crunching Gravel: On Growing Up in the Thirties; For You, Lili Marlene;* and *A Night With the Undertaker's Grandson.*

Parts Three through Five emphasize love and marriage. "Gary" represents less than half of *Cool Zebras of Light*, out of print since the late '70's when the press publishing the book was destroyed in a canyon fire in Santa Barbara. Its appearance here, I hope, will give it a renewed life. Gary, a loving, turbulent soul, committed suicide in 1974.

Most of "Marriage" is derived from *The Drowned Man to the Fish*. With "Gary," these poems reflect a difficult period in my life, resolved with Paul Trachtenberg, himself a fine poet, archivist, director, and editor. We are celebrating our twentieth anniversary. "Paul" contains poems celebrating this friendship. Most were written in 1987 and revised considerably since then. A trio of poems on King Ludwig of Bavaria arise from my numerous performances as the mad king. Trachtenberg produced, directed, and served as technician and publicist. I warn the reader that not every fact, person, and incident in "Gary," "Marriage," and "Paul" actually occurred.

Part Six contains "Gordon at Khartoum," my first poem to be published in an international magazine, the Canadian *The Fiddlehead*, in 1960. The earliest poems of all were a pair very derivative of the Victorians that appeared in 1948, in an obscure monograph, *Contemporary Poets of Wisconsin*. Little did I know then that my interest in historical figures would lead to half a dozen book-length verse portraits. "For Jeff," first published in *The Reaper*, in 1987, is a departure for me in tone and style. The newest poems of all, "The Murderer," "Elderly Dying AIDS Victim," and "Love on the Frontier," are in a recent style, which, as the reader will see, relate to the pop/op/surrealist styles of *Holy Cow: Parable Poems*.

"Van Gogh to Gauguin," which I care greatly for, was the title poem for *Gauguin's Chair: Selected Poems*. The poem, I hope, encapsulates the strands of love, paternal, fraternal, and aesthetic, that inform most of my work. On a trip to Amsterdam, almost overwhelmed by personal distress, I visited the Van Gogh Museum. In the vivid slashes of purple paint applied by Van Gogh, I saw my own undergoing as well.I left the Museum better prepared to abandon some of my self-obsessions.

Part Seven samples my eight persona books: the subjects include both male and female saints and murderers. Some of these reflect my period of academic expertise, nineteenth century British culture, with a special emphasis on the Victorians, about and from whom I have also published criticism, scholarship, and editions of letters.

I have many people to thank, including the editors who over the years have had faith in my work. A special thanks to Melissa Mytinger,

John and Elaine Gill, Bill Truesdale, Pamela and Charles Plymell, Felice Picano, Anselm Parlatore, Teo Savory, Alan Brilliant, Bill Warner, and to Wayne State University, W. W. Norton, Inc., Liveright, Inc., and New Rivers for keeping my books in print for as long as they have. I hope they will approve of these new incarnations. My surviving children Rob II, Meredith, and Jefferson, who have not enjoyed the world's most conventional father, deserve many embraces, as does Paul Trachtenberg for his caring and affection. I am a blest man. Finally, a special word of thanks to Charles Hood who has generously supported most of my efforts with friendship and acute critical attention.

— *Robert Peters*

I: RICHARD

Wings without feathers creaking in the sun,
The close dirt dancing on a sunless stone
God's night and day: down this space He has smiled,
O who would take the vision from the child?

—Theodore Roethke

THEME

I call your name, son,
festooned and touched
with amber in my mind:
Richard. Peace.

The apple turns to ash.
The slumbering worm
begins to swell, stir,
prepares his rubbery mouth
for the assault.

I run a cinder through my palm,
firing the ember

and my flesh burns as
heart drains its fear—
flick of a worm's beak.

These are fragments of pain,
stalactites of the heart
doomed to melt, leveling
panic, the jab in the guts,
the slick vein leaping
over my hand, perplexed,
sick, over its branchings
multiform.

The sun comes down.
It stamps its lamp
against my brain.
I shielded, shield my eyes
against the glare! Where
are you gone, son?
Where? Where?

MOTIF

In winter
a bird drops from a bough.
The snow entombs him
wraps him in.

In spring
feathers stiffen.
Wings collapse.
Pin oil grease
thaws and dries.
The beak whitens.
Eye juice melts.
Flesh softens—
a purple stain.

TRANSFORMATION

Between death's hot coppery sides
the slime of birth becomes
a chalky track of bone
compressed in time to slate,
or gneiss, or marble—
pressed lifeless into stone.

They will never remember
one so young, or one so mirthful,
or one so quiet in his bed.

SONG FOR A SON

My son's image was painted on sand.
The wind from off the lake
bears no news of him
or of his impression.

Was it arrogance to think
I could hold his features?

I had set them in memory,
fashioned cameos for the mind,
had seen that face at will
in various attitudes, transforming me
when he was alive.

But I am blind!
Unable to create a brow,
a lash, the hollow down
the back of the neck,
the throat!

Look.
Those trees hold nothing in their branches.
Those rushes by the lake
so rife with blackbirds
hold nothing:
          Mist faces,
          faces in shrouds...
          faces in clouds...
Water has worn the cameos down.

PRESERVE

That mass of trees:
moist veins racked against the sky,
mortal backdrop
for a world of twig, black leaf
and large hill riddled
with mange and rot.

Beneath your feet
a bridge, snowy,
with crisp flakes
spun from the hooves of does
in troll-land
anxious for their young.

There, dazzled
by blue light, by ice,
you sped through the morning:
your boot buckles clicking
and red mittens pointing
(hands on film)
toward each frozen
wonder of the trail:

globs of cow fat tied in mesh
stuck with seeds
(corn, oat, sunflower, rice)
swung from branches.
Coconut skulls filled with meal,
fists of oak, wood-knobs greased,
orange rinds, and powdered milk in bottles—
all to nourish the birds.

Sparrows shivered as we passed.
And on you ran.

I called out to you,
called out to you, boy,
saw your prints and joy
skim through the water
spin like the bugs of summer
on the drugged lake
we flung pebbles at,
begged time to flounder.

On you sped
through woods and brush
passed the pike weed marsh,
the beaver dam.

I caught your sparkle
toward the rounding bay
drenched with sun, fisherman.

"Keep, keep within sight of land,"
I cried; "of every riddle, joy,
the pains of Christmas, Easter,
grandma's house, the fair"—
the prompting died.

"The enemy!" you screamed
and with your sister
leaped the brook
a month before the close,
before
        the trap sprang
before
        the ice rang in
        and froze your mouth, heart,
        glorious eyes and limbs:
        ice flowers of death,
        blue, exfoliate utterly!

SNOW

I shall never touch snow
and not see your plaid coat
and the blue cap
with flaps like small rabbits
by your ears.

REPORT

I turned you, Richard,
kissed your neck
to wake you from
that fever-breaking sleep
and saw
your blue cracked lip
the stark death mark.

HOSPITAL

Wheeze away, O green steel tank!
Breathe, gray nose cup set
over the hardening cartilage
of his nose!
>   (Unsheeted form
>   on a wheeled-in table;
>   robe, fresh urine stain
>   on the pajamas—designs
>   of tugboats, bedroom
>   slippers).

Mechanical sustainer! Push those lungs,
inflate them, swell them! Shock them
into breath again!
>   (Bent heads
>   hands probing
>   detecting
>   over the wheeled-in
>   table).

O neutral doctor! O delicate finger
laboring! O pluck the heart (fat
and vein) blood-fretted jewel,
strum melody!

>   (He does not breathe!)

Dredge out the heart
and shake it, slap it, bathe it
in the glare
of the stainless light
above the table.
Massage it   prick it
be brutal, hand, be God

prick the quiescent

                             immobile

                                   gem.

WALL

Let's wait beside
the nonsense wall, all dread:
white flaking bricks
dust for tears,
for scissors, paste.

"Spratt and wife," I say
to call you back. "Cow,
dog, moon, and spoon."
I try again.
"Burst, fat, hungering George
who flew away, was never seen."
I assume a troll's voice:
"The Human Pole, a string of a man
with all his buttons lost, Tucker
wanting supper, the stolen tarts,
the Jack of Hearts snapped flat
against the deck, breaded honey,
blackbird, the nurse's blear
proboscis stuck to an icy line,
Riding Hood's basket
adorned with silk, with milk,
the wolf's meal, the squeal,
and grandma freed—
grotesque and happy birth!"

MORNING

In the first sift of gray light
the first cars rumbling
I stand, glance toward the yard
past the trellis where you played
turned stones for worms,
to the swings, the seats
you painted, splattering
the cracked planks
and the chinning bar
with gold, to the gay
slab boats and the machines
built from magazines
torn, pasted, placed
on stilts of Tinker Toys
and brown blocks
propped by rocks,
to the mix you stirred
that fatal morning
seated under the leafless oak:
Porridge, you exclaimed,
magic food
meant to sprout trees of ice cream,
balloon flowers, crayons,
mice, gilt shrubs and wishbones,
kittens, dogs.

Dawn strikes the oak.
Gloss sheens the lake,
spring's tulip-hue.

(And there is the sand.
The tunnels for the mice
are still intact. The

twigs for trees
you stuck in mousetown
wait for spring.)

A pool glistens
near the ageratum:
winter's drizzle,
chill sterility.

EASTER

Meredith gave up her doll last night.
You would not have known his face,
so aged it was. Soap
was hopeless. His rag cheeks
were cancerous.
His lips, still smiling, mocked decay.
Raggedy Andy, Raggedy Andy.
Meredith wrote a note:
"Spirit him off to Easterland."
She kissed him.
"One more day to live. One more night."
She left him in his chair.
By morning he disappeared.

Play with him, Richard.
Keep his gray face.
Kiss all death from his button eyes.
Kiss sleep from his mouth.
Meredith asks it.

FERN, MOTH, AND HAND

The fern molds into bits,
syllables spewed
upon the yeasty earth,
spoors. The tattered leaves
boast tips of red. Nearby,
an orange fallow bulb
lures a crisp moth
(the moth is scorched)
to the pale, buttery stem.
He flutters, bruised eye,
antenna crippled—
a stick half broken under water.
Bubbles pass as the tail curls
toward the startled, vanquished eye.
Red chaff crumbles.
Cheese from the spoor-head follows.
The flesh stem splinters.
The eye dies, the wing's eye
dissolves, the antennae shake,
straighten, clapped shut.

Son, who cast the stone?
Whose wrist flexed the muscle?
What have we lost, son?
Can you say, son?
Son, can you say?

BOAT

A petal from a saffron bell
drops from a bush. My image
rushes after the oar.
My hook trails free.
Then, fearing the depths
I pull toward shore.
The wind moves.
Broad skies move.
A dour partridge floats
above the fox's wet nose.
A dragonfly quivers in a web
jewelled with wing debris.

The boat is beached.
(The boat is bleached).
Oars rest on the seat.
A fish splatters behind me
where the water gathers.

"Fish." I grasp its sides.

There is blood.
I have ripped a finger.
A red pearl drops into the water.
Sweet blood. Our sweet blood.

FEVER

We did not seek this monument,
nor ever wish it:
bed, drawn shade,
steamer vaporizing the room,
peeling the sill,
the lungs (slender ferny tracks
born of an ancient sea),
and fever, loathsome traveler
with his pack all rolled,
his blanket ready for a tryst,
a true fire, reedy,
igniting his destination
our dear son's capitol,
his brain.

TURTLES AND MICE

As we box up your coat, son,
your laces, rusty skates,
and the black stuffed seal
who truly died beside you
hugged beneath your stiffening arm,
and seek you in those squiggles
you made on paper, the turtles
you cut out, bent the legs of
so they'd walk, and placed them

on a toy farm with mice, blind,
a troll waits,
his spiked head facing west,
his eyes sapphires in the dark.

DANCE

A brain danced in the wind.
A natural shape for a natural mind—
its motions diaphanous.
Outrageous performer!
    No rod, stick, string
    or invisible hand.
Clouds rose behind it.

Music I could not hear
(but only imagined)
whirled into sound:
tunes for an oboe
tambourine and violin.
A brain danced in the wind.

There were no trees at hand.
Birds settled to earth
and slept on warm stones
wing-fast. A brain
danced in the wind.

OH, CABIN MICE!

Frenzied by the smell
of stale bread, jam,
and meat locked up
for the season, cabin mice
scamper over carpets,
up and down cupboards,
beat paths around the fireplace,
discover envelopes of grain,
poisoned pellets
prepared for them.

They ignore tails
and whiskers, female heat,
lice in their fur, the
snow water near the door,
decree sharp teeth,
squeal, squirm, nip
and draw mouse blood,
sate themselves,
grow tranquil, serene,
tummied (the tits
of the mother mice
bursting with milk),
make lingering copulations.
Then:
the advent of slow blood,
deterioration of cell walls,
hemophilia falsely induced,
the swelling up of hot breath,
charred lungs, blood seeping
as a bright aster forms at the mouth,
as fallen oak leaves bloom
in the snow

and a calendula of blood blooms
beneath the whipping tail.

KITTENS

The kittens came tonight,
the ones you'd wished for
when you broke
the hen's breast bone
that Wednesday, death day
morning. You had asked for
plump dark woolly cats
with eyes like olives, glossy,
cats tumbling on the floor
soundless, pricking at string,
lapping up blue milk,
their abdomens as tight as udders.

This was the scene:
the brindled cat squirmed
beneath the chair,
whined, rose, and plunged
spread-legged through the room
to find a box, a hat,
a place by a commode for birth.
We set a blue crate for her,
spread down a towel and waited.
Two shaky forms appeared
smeared with blood,
fur like wet licorice,

eyelids swollen.
The mother screamed
(an angry rip of cloth),
glanced swiftly back,
impelled by burning muscle
found the wet cowering lumps,
peeled then swallowed
their rubbery translucent
coats, lent her tongue
to smear the wobbling
panting forms all shiny
bound with feebleness.
Ink black they fell
into a land of honey.
Then dropped the third,
and last.

But earlier, on wish-day
death-day, poised
on my mound of sand,
I'd said: "No cats,"
and quelled your joy
with news of chance
loose from the zoo
against you. "No mice,
no toads, no turtles,
salamanders, frogs"—
I made a catalogue.
"They die. Their little toes
curl up like leaves,
their waxy eyes go shut,
their tails hang limp,
their whiskers droop."

Dreading each death's advent,
I sought to spare you.

Each lost pet might break
deep, deep within your heart,
might crystallize its
red wet velvet sides
into long beads of rice
to feed the worm—
or snap them into tears,
like seeds, to break on stone:
each death a buzz,
an eel's tail slapped
against your knee,
a blue, a fatal jolt!

In proof I said,
"Count up your pets:
the molting snake
gashed half way to its tail,
remember him?" We speared Snake food
(some, living, bled on toothpicks)
and thrust the gobbets
past the forked and flicking palate,
the svelte unhinging jaws.
But Snake, rolled like an earthworm
in his leaves, was dead.

Then Mouse: remember
how you bore him through the yard
wrapped in his hard leaf shroud,
his green tail
sprinkling mortality
like ivy juice
all over you that day?
You brought a metal pail,
spilled water in the hole
torn by your rusted shovel.
You wept and gracefully

placed Mouse beneath a tulip root.
Two nails formed a cross,
a fallen leaf the savior.
There Mouse still lies
set by your own hands
firmly into place—
unless the earth
with acid formed from oaks
has decomposed his bones,
like yours, to ash,
and slipped all down
between packed quartzite,
sandstone, beryl,
smoothed out with lime
and all the other flavors
of an earthy crypt.

But all my scare of zoo
and deep-felled nightmare
failed, and would not settle
in your brain's mailed
small hole for fear,
where clung invisible
the hung smoke
of the sleeping fatal fever.
I smiled broadly from the table,
hitched up my belt,
enjoyed your innocence,
bade you break the bone
and gladly eat your wish.

With shy delight
you seized the dish,
took up and sprung the wing,

turned it like stone
to see through in the light,
sprung it wide, asked it to snap:

Jarring the light-hung
particles of dust
caught near the window
the bone did break!

Our house now crawls with kittens.
They tumble, stumble, run,
find bits of sun, find mother's
udders, mews. They lick themselves,
waver on infirm claws,
do all the acts you knew
live kittens make.

I'm glad you took these facts
with you into the night.
I'd rather have you take
these kitten facts along
than all the history
you never came to know,
the shouts of passion, war,
the violence of cars, the poetry
that never broke itself against your ears.
O, that there had been more!

THE BURIAL OF THE ASHES

1.

I take you from the church
in a brown leathery cube.
I cannot read the label,
the facts of ash.
A car, passing
throws sun against my face—
a clarion.

I ask for a shovel.
"No trouble," says the preacher.
I follow, pass through Gethsemane.

We have trouble with the shovel:
gone from its place,
a plain fact askew.

I fear that the winds
will howl soundless again.

We find a spade,
though not the one we wished,
and I lead the way
to a bush on a rolling slope
set with rock
like the fringe of a well.
The crown of the green bush wavers.

I open the box: a sack, translucent
crammed with scraps of
brown black white and yellow bone.

I test the weight, press the sack
to my check, hold it to my eyes.

Sun streams through, turns
that ivory to gold
that pale pale white to blue,
those bits of brown to red!

2.

I break the earth
(the spade moves well):
I prune a root
and smooth the hole.
I press the earth by hand,
drop in a leaf, and kneel.
I crumble-in loam.
As grains slip through
I hunger to count them,
I hunger to count them.

I hope for silence,
vision, a shimmering saint
bearing a twig studded with
emeralds, a gift.

Richard, Richard,
there was snow that day
and sun enough to dazzle empires
when you ran laughing
beside the frosty lake,
mortal, lovely, mine.

CAT, WORD, AND FERN

Words roll over,
their feet in air, clawing
the turbulent heart.
O heart!
The claws stiffen, curl
like fern fronds.
The fern molds.
The words die, they die.

THE BEACH

And now,
wherever I walk
heel and sole print
(salt drenched),
stir the
rotted eye stalks
of lobsters, crunch
marooned shells...
Look! There's a creature
on the beach, brine
gone forever. Purple arms,
six at least, all furious,
hoist the body.
The arms flare
as the creature swells,
shoots forth ink,
curls its tentacles, bursts,
becomes a glob
which the sun will erase.
It grows extinct,
is not.

CODA

1.

Stars burst,
pin back the sable
for a glance, then fade.

Petals drop from the vine
and the pink grape blackens,
the fig contains the worm,
leaves yellow and drop.
Rust swallows the metal frames
supporting.

Beside the lake the beaver
slap their tails. In the deep lake
fish glimmer. On the water
wild geese wait. Tomorrow
their keen breasts shall beat
streams of stars.

You loved it here!

2.

Our thrusts are scarcely marble,
they crumble. There is
no private art: we write what we can.
Our leapings fade, so does
our burbling mirth.
Our begging and begetting,
they too pass over
the fury of the hour.

What we seek, what binds us,

is a wish to share with
sleek beasts waiting in the fields,
all turned head to head,
toward the waning sun,
a semblance of calm.

Richard Nathaniel Frank Peters:
Sept. 18, 1955-Feb. 10, 1960.

II: ORIGINS

Long I was hugg'd close—long and long.

—Walt Whitman

EAGLE RIVER, WISCONSIN: 1930

Gangsters came to Eagle River
but not one singer, writer, or painter.
I can show you
where Dillinger sweated at little Bohemia
where Mayor Kelly rubbed his belly
and shot well body guarded rounds of golf
where Capone's crew sniffed danger
adjusted their knickers
masqueraded as berry pickers
in the less ominous air of Eagle River
when the Chicago home zoo grew too hot.
And governors La Follette and Heil
paused awhile
patted their wallets
observed the wild blueberry crop
gathered votes
were startled to note
so few folk
in that beautiful backwoods
of logged off, mined out land,
while Herbert Hoover
chose the Brule for hooking trout,
saw Eagle River as nothing to shout about.

And yet one could/can
flounder
up to his eyes there,
and the mind could/can
blunder frenzied there,
poems choking the throat.

MY FATHER AS HOUSE BUILDER

Cedar poles skidded by horse
from swamp to highland, stripped
of bark, hauled to the house-site
on a knoll near the county road.
A pattern in the sand
for two rooms and kitchen, drawn
with a sapling and a string.
Cedar poles adzed flat,
other poles notched for walls.
We chinked logs with swamp moss
secured by slats, then plastered.
We puttied the windows.
Scrap lumber for the roof and floors.
A cellar hole in the living room,
the sand fetched up by buckets
and dumped in a marsh hole
filled in for a garden plot.
The upper story, hip-roofed, low,
built without plumb lines.
Tin smoke-pipe leaning north,
tied by guy wires to the roof.
We nagged Dad to finish the walls,
but he never did.
The studs, he said,
were good for hanging pots and clothes.
The walls we insulated
with flattened cardboard boxes
and decorated them with pictures
cut from Hearst's *American Weekly Sunday News.*

MOTHER

Girl, sixteen,
straining over a washtub
in an ice shed of a house
chinked with moss
veiled with tar paper.

House alive with mice
in warm weather,
in cold with ice.

Your stuttering wash lines
strung up
through the house:
slab underwear (flat
salted fillets) sheets,
shirts, board-stiff
dresses, nightshirts.

And the meals: pancakes
whipped out of batter
kept in a crock
fermenting on the back
of the wood stove.
Peanut butter (County Welfare)
extended by blending
bacon drippings.

Repeat those gestures!
Strip away all subsequent events!
Goad us to the pasture,
to the starved potato field
and the bean field
while you prod, curse your life,
as night, a peddlar,

drops poisoned seed,
and a wreathing fog settles in,
soft underbelly, soft thighs,
tight against the throat
dark lovely throat of winter!
I crouch again, waiting,
hoping you are near.
Touch me!

SNAPSHOTS WITH BUCK, MODEL-A FORD, AND KITCHEN

1.

The buck's neck in a twist beside the car's head lamp.
His tongue sticky, pimpled cardboard.
Gashed throat. Eye glassed over.
Belly slit, incision swept with blood-hair.
Hooves secured with a rope.
Magnificent twelve-pronged antlers.

2.

Dad whetted a knife on an emery stone.
A galvanized tub caught the dribbles.
He sliced off the head, disjointing the neck bone.

The severed hooves he placed on paper
under the pot-bellied stove.
He shucked the hide,
would later treat it with lye
and cure it for mittens.

Grease in the black spider sizzled.
Dad pushed his thumbs into the savory venison.
Discs of marrow-bone for soup.
Piles of purple meat for grinding.

We buried the venison on the snowy roof,
to be eaten as needed.
Morning, tracks circled the house.
Maddened by spoor, wolves
had snapped at their heels all night.

FEW OF US FEEL SAFE
ANYWHERE

He recalls
digging up mole routes
in a country school yard.
The mangy grass
bound and flattened by mud
arose beneath soft channels
burrowed by mole snouts.

He unearthed a fertile nest,
fought down two friends
to keep the blind pink furless
creatures between his hands.

He won by running up to teacher,
intending to present her
with those jewels, his catch,
a quest, possession all his own,
for her, his lover.

But others watched, grinned
as he drew apart those palms,
revealed those pinkish forms,
stilled, calm, their shanks
of legs drawn up beneath
their toothless jaws, their
whiskers bent, their mouths
each bearing blood.

MISCARRIAGE

My mother bathes alone—
the metal tub,
the kettle of hot water,
on a strip of carpet, in her room.

She has lost another child.
Dad buries it under the birches
near the well.

God is on her side.
She didn't want the child.
He listened to her when she cried.
He opened a fresh wound wide
in His eternal side.
The baby slipped in and hid there
when he died.

SMUDGE-POT

Mosquitoes
plague the house at dusk.

They bite you,
plump with blood
resemble
small overloaded tubers.

They float to the nearest twig.
The welts they've raised
burn and tingle.

DOCTOR

He was drunk, and his breath stunk.
He wore a brown wool suit and a tan coat.
His brusque voice demanded water,
towels, and a small brush.
His hands fluttered when he said
the birth looked foul.
The cord was strangling the baby's throat.
If he failed to cry, he would die.

I saw the red body in the air.
It had black hair.

The Doctor waved us off—
"Wait in the kitchen," he said.
"We'll clean up now. The boy's fine.
We'll be done in no time."

We sat across the table.
The kerosene lamp stood in the middle.
My sister was staring at her knuckles.
I saw her skinny breasts, her brown hair braid,
her firm lips. She looked at me.
I thought she would cry.
I didn't know why.

PIG-FAMILY GAME

I was the sow, she was the boar.
Six kitchen chairs for a pen.
We put on winter coats and grunted.
I lay on my side, coat open
and birthed six pigs.
Only one was a runt. Six squirts,
minimal pain, minimal swelling.
I peeled the after-births,
then nudged the piglets into standing.
Boar was in a corner plowing up edible roots.
Sow ate the placentas.
The piglets yanked and nuzzled her teats.
Sow milk ran, her ovaries tingled.
There was froth on her mouth,
in the black juicy loam of the pen.

THE SECRET

That he would be a man
was in God's plan.
He was adept at chopping wood
and milking cows. He cared for the hens,
talked dirty with the boys at school,
adeptly used his dad's tools,
imagined the family he would sire,
sold garden seeds and picture wire.
He fondled girls' breasts in his dreams,
expressed his guilt in dank night-screams,

watched his cousin Grace at the lake disrobe,
went along with the homophobes.

HOT BREAD

He stands by a gravel pit
staring at Clark Gable, shirtless,
wearing dark glasses.

When he comes, the hole in his heart
pains more than before:
He can't go West! He can't study law!
He can't teach or sing! He can't do anything!

He wipes himself with maple leaves.
He smells fresh bread.
In the kitchen he knows
that a half is enough,
the raisin, or the unmilled flour
of the hot, sweet loaf.

POTATO BUGS

Dad paid us a nickel a quart to pick the bugs.
The plants, just blossoming, were infested.
By dropping the bugs into a jar
they didn't juice our fingers.
They exuded a noisome odor.

When Dad paid us
we drained the kerosene to use again,
dumped the dead bugs on the compost heap.

NIGHT SOIL

It was always this way:
  each spring Dad shovelled up
  outhouse winter deposits.

He dug into the pile from the rear,
  shovelled it onto a stone boat
  hauled it to the fields,
  with my uncle's horse.

Pages torn from Sears catalogues
  stuck to the soil, patchwork of
  men and boys in underwear,
  cheap suits, overalls, tough boots and bluchers.

Dad claimed he knew each Saturday's deposit,
  when we crunched peanuts, played cards,
  and listened to the Hit Parade.

He strewed the offal over the fields,
  then plowed it under. The disk
  restored some to the surface

Where squash and corn grew large and green
  sprouting from night soil
  rich, rich ordure, rich and human.

RAT

1.

Dad raised the cellar door,
shot down a light, caught the creature
in the beam, on a pile of sand.
Milky potato roots writhed
up the loam walls.
I saw the yellow teeth.

2.

Dad built a trap from an apple crate.
Smoke erased our human smell.
We threw in some wheat. A rigged door.
We waited for the trap to latch,
for the rat to screech.
At midnight we went to bed.

3.

Next morning Dad left for work
on the WPA crew. Nothing new
in the cellar. "He's too smart,"
Dad said. "We'll have to shoot him."

4.

I was stoking the wood stove fire...
Mom rushed in from the kitchen.
"We've caught him!" she shouted.

5.

I raised the trap.
The rat plunged and snarled.
He gnawed the wood.
He bit the chicken wire.

We removed the stove's top lid
and slid the trap over the flames.
I opened the trap.
I beat the rat's toes with a poker.
I struck his teeth.
He fell into the fire.

RITES OF PASSAGE

1.

Snow patches.
Stone marrow, ferny maiden hair.
Faint rubbery cranberry buds,
at dusk. Star flower moss.
Mist-swallowing water steaming,
welling from whirling and ashes,
subterranean
limpid and potent,
sexual flow and current.

2.

Coyotes yipped and howled.
Fir trees cracked with cold.
Moonlight flashed snow.
A stream spewed ice, gurgled
and flowed. Blue-ice stars
swung within reach. A teal cloud
covered the moon.
Vertical tiers of magnificent
northern lights!

THE BUTCHERING

1.

Dad told me to hold the knife
and the pan. I heard the click
on wood of the bullet inserted,
rammed. Saw a flicker thrash
in a tree beside the trough,
saw a grain in the sow's mouth,
felt my guts slosh.

"Stand back," dad said.
Waffled snow track
pressed by his boots and mine.
Blood and foam. "Keep the knife
sharp, son, and hold the pan."
One of us had shuffled,
tramped a design,
feet near the jack pine.
"She'll bleed slow.
Catch all the blood you can."

A rose unfolded, froze.
"Can't we wait?" I said.
"It should turn warmer."

Spark, spark buzzing
in the dark.

"It's time," dad said, and waited.

2.

Bless all this beauty! preacher
had exclaimed, *all sin and beauty
in this world! Beast and innocent!*

Fist bones gripped the foreshortened
pulpit rim. Thick glasses
drove his furious pupils in.

3.

Dad brought the rifle to the skull.
The sow's nose plunged into the swill,
the tips of her white tallow ears as well.
Splunk! Straight through the brain, suet
and shell. Stunned! Discharge of food,
bran. Twitch of an ear. Potato, carrot,
turnip slab. "Quick. The knife. The pan."

He sliced the throat.
The eye closed over.
Hairy ears stood up, collapsed.
Her blood soured into gelatin.
She had begun to shit.

4.

We dragged her
to the block and tackle rig.
We tied her tendons, raised her,
sloshed her up and down.
We shaved her hair,
spun her around, cut off
her feet and knuckles,
hacked off her head,
slashed her belly
from asshole down through
bleached fat throat.
Jewels spilled out
crotches of arteries
fluids danced and ran.

We hoisted her out of dog reach
dumped her entrails in the snow
left the head for the dogs to eat—
my mother disliked head-meat.
The liver, steaming, monochrome,
quivered with eyes.
We took it home.

5.

I went to my room.
Tongues licked my neck.
I spread my arms,
threw back my head.
The tendons of a heel snapped.
What had I lost?
Bit   bridle   rage?

Preacher in his pulpit
fiddling, vestments aflame.
He, blazing, stepping down
to me. Hot piss came.
I knelt on the floor,
bent over, head in arms.
Piss washed down, more.
I clasped my loins,
arm crossed over arm.
And I cried, loving my guts,
O vulnerable guts,
guts of creatures.

THE SOW'S HEAD

The day was like pewter.
The gray lake a coat
open at the throat. The border
of trees—frayed mantle collar,
hairs, evergreen. The sky dun.
Chilling breeze. Hem of winter.

I passed the iodine-colored brook,
hard waters open,
the weight of the sow's head
an ache from shoulder to waist,
the crook of my elbow numb.
Juices seeping through
the wrapping paper.

I was wrong to take it.
There were meals in it.
I would, dad said,
assist with slaughter,
scrape off hair, gather blood.
I would be whipped
for thieving from the dogs.

I crossed ice
which shivered, shone.
No heads below, none,
nor groans—only water, deep,
and the mud beds of frogs asleep.
Not a bush quivered,
not a stone. Snow.

Old snow had formed
hard swirls bone
and planes with

wind whipped ridges
for walking upon.
And beneath, in the deep,
bass quiet, perch whirling fins,
bluegills, sunfish dim-eyed
soaking heat. Mud
would be soft down there,
rich, tan, deeper than a man:
silt of leeches, leaves
tumbling in from trees,
loon feces, mulch-thick
mudquick, and lignite forming,
cells rumbling, rifts.

I knelt, chopped through
layers of ice until water, pus,
spilled up, choking the wound.
I widened the gash.
Tchick! Tchick!
Chips of ice flew.
Water blew from the hole,
the well, a whale, expired.
My knees were stuck to the ice.

I unwrapped the paper.
The head appeared
shorn of its beard.
Its ears stood up. The snout
with its Tinker Toy holes held blood.
Its eyes were shut.
There was grain on its mouth.

It sat on the snow
as though it lived below,
leviathan come for air
limbs and hulk

dumb to my presence there.

I raised the sow's head
by its ears. I held it
over the hole, let it go,
watched it sink, a glimmer
of pink, a wink of a match
an eyelid. . .

A bone in my side beat.

THE LAKE

The lake is anvil-shaped,
its edges roughened, off-center,
as the boys said it was,
the boys who fished there
each summer, who boasted later
boys from town
with their own canoes
bought, not built like mine,
pretested on the water.

In the mind:
crippled trees—a brainful.
The lake is a shape, in a haze,
a rasping wind. Shore foliage
and water weeds.

No one will find you here.

THAT FAMILY

That family had ten kids. They bred like rabbits.

That family ate with their fingers from pots and pans
of venison and beans.

That family tapped maple trees for sap, fished and hunted
in all seasons.

That family never wiped their asses—they had no paper.

That family slept four to a bed, the girls slept with their
parents.

That family tied up the oldest brother's morning erection,
hooked the string to the ceiling, woke him with a jerk,
induced ejaculation.

That family—the mother had great breasts, a hairy chin,
and owned a single purple dress secured with safety pins.

That family played pinochle, poker, and 500 rummy.
They never went to church or believed in the Easter Bunny.

That family worked at the saw mill, swilled booze, had fights
and went to jail.

That family took me fishing, taught me sex in the barn,
and invited me swimming. We flashed our asses
at the girls.

I loved that family. They were fantasy country,
somewhere south of Eden, north of Daniel's den.

LUCY ROBINSON

Lucy Robinson's rimless spectacles
rode athwart her nose.
About her neck were chunks of fur
which made it appear
that she had tiny rabbits on.
Masses of hair hung down her face
(old curtains belted low
about the waist).
Her wrists were fat.
Her hands were knobs,
the knuckles bumps and knots
which creaked to open.
Her mouth seldom parted when she spoke.

Through the musty curtains
she appeared,
shattering the sleep of moths,
hums of flies, raising dust.

Massive creature
keeping the shoe store
in her decayed parlor,
selling one pair a day,
two before school began
and more for Santa Claus.

She fetches a box
from a shelf behind a cage.
Dad pulls me up,
points to a brightening shoe.

Lucy wheezes and the light is dim.
Her arthritic finger latches in
behind my heel. A dead bird.
I feel its bill.

I want her hand free!
The size to be right!
The shoes will pinch and blister.
I'll have to break them in evenings
drawing water for the cows!

She stuffs our dollars
into the tight mouse of her hand.
Whiskers on her knuckles twitch
and whiskers on her mouth.

In that debris, in the dust now
an image glows, a lamp wink,
a jewel, a gland (faint radium pulse),
a spotted lung, striations on a hand,
an arthritic spur, a quivering claw....

What have you done, Lucy Robinson?

AUNT

I found her in bed
with the covers thrown back
and a hole the size of
a fish's sphincter ripped
below her navel.
A folded rose of pain
rubbed smut against her.
"He did it," she screamed.
"The son of a bitch!"

We found her revolver
under the wood pile
where she'd thrown it.
We found it the next afternoon.

TOMMY McQUAKER

Tommy McQuaker's soft fat dad
clerked at the bank.
His bosomy mother Pearl prattled.
Her orange hair was tightly curled.

In summer, Tommy
swished down Main Street
with a poodle on a leash.
He wore shorts, sandals,
and a polkadot tie.

We said he lacked balls
that he cupped his hands when he peed.
He was into theater and verse.
He had a "boyfriend" in Chicago.
That town's exotic.

I kept my distance from him,
as I did from Catholic nuns,
on the far side of the street.

I feared Tommy would bite my lips
and bestow awesome diseases.
I craved his obscene squeezes.

ALBERT

He was as hated as a runted shoat.
He was his mother's not his dad's. He wore no colored coat.
They beat him with horse harness, as they would.
They called him bastard, and told him to be good.

He had to do chores, as the younger brother said,
and hoe the corn and chop the firewood.
Whenever he went alone to the lake for swimming,
they waited to give him another vicious trimming.

He smiled at strangers, excelled at school,
was liked by the teachers and the principal.
He was lithe and tall, with jet-black eyes and hair.
Girls stared, giggled, and wrote mash notes in the air.

He clerked at Holperin's grocery one summer.
His folks took half his money.
He bought a Model-T, gabardine pants, a shirt and tie,
a 21-rifle, and a strong light to check his beaver traps by.

That winter he shot two bucks for food,
and hooked several large pike, fishing through the ice.
He chopped half the winter's wood.
When they killed the sow he caught the blood.

Spring came. A row over the plowing.
He was needed at the store and begged off farming.
His half-brother Jim chased him with an axe,
screaming he would kill him.

His leg was hacked. Bone-pain shimmered.
He grappled with his brother. His mother
splintered the axe over his back.
He slumped, rose, then freed himself.

He ran through the trees beyond the meadow.
He swam in the icy lake out past the middle,
dove, retrieved handfuls of muck
and when he was spent, returned home.

He strode past the men who were plowing
and entered the house. He ignored his mother shouting,
grabbed his rifle, inserted a shell,
declared he would shoot himself, down by the well.

"You won't!" his mother screamed, barring the door.
He shoved her aside and cocked the gun.
She watched through the window glass.
He bled to death in the deep green grass.

THE PROM

I asked her to the dance
then ran from school, from home,
from my ugly clothes.

I gave her gardenias.
Pinned them clumsily to her clothes.

She would not dance with me.
"I won't be seen," she said,
"stumbling and fumbling."

I ran five miles home,
five miles to my bed,
five miles
to the quilt thrown over my head.

ROSE MARIE, I LOVE YOU

1.

At twelve
I had myself baptized
induced my family to attend church
taught Sunday School
mowed down various
adolescent heresies
with the jawbone of my zeal,
sang Solomon's song
and erotic hymns,
savored the cannibalism
of wafer and wine, made
the Savior's wounds my own,
displayed myself upon crosses,
prayed during onanistic sweats,
during pounding thunderstorms,
dressed in a sheet,
communed with my lover,
saw the world entirely as glass.

2.

To walk three miles
on a Sunday, a hick boy
strewn with the ids
of his ancestors,
to see his first movie
Rose Marie I Love You.
Warbling away
those singers
smothered mountains
with layers of chocolate sound.

But my mother's hats were not Jeanette's.
And I never saw my Dad,
straw boss of a WPA crew,
lead his men, shovel over shoulder,
sing out his lungs
in a hairy-chested marching song.

UNCLES

1.

My uncles were gassed in the trenches,
pissed out their fear in the trenches,
saw horses blown to scrap,
dragged comrades from bardedwire traps
fought off bronze rats
in Ypres, Belleau Wood,
Chateau-Thierrey, Verdun.

2.

Trailing piss, my uncles run
nowhere
to place hands   nowhere
to insert wound-rags   nowhere
to scream, blare, claw smoke
nowhere
to latch the mask, no nose
to hang it from, throat,
lingam shot away. Shapes
dangle from bones,
running, running this way,
running.

CANOE JOURNEY

1.

The canoe
slides easily down
from the top
of the Model-A Ford.

I launch it
regard the trees
shivering aspen
huddling wall.

Is there blood?

I see head lamp eyes,
saliva, and a hairy jaw.
My dad's tracks race
through the woods.

2.

My knees press against
the metal moldridge of the sides.

A bursting river
swollen now
where water
newly freed from ice
is glazed
by an oleaginous dark.

If I could reach bottom
and rend that cluster
of underwater garnets
broken on granite!

3.

I pass demolished trees
where a storm
has splattered them.
Debris is kindling-spun.

I slide beneath
tamarack and spruce.

The dipping of a spoon
into a spring full of water.

Grabbing branches
I slide the boat along
pass through
a bronchial tangle,
heart system.

The air is sweet with
alcohol and blood,
no houses near, no farms,
entirely deserted.

I reach a meadow,
faint frozen green,
red moss spoor,
the sky smoky,
anger in the clouds,
blue, a dram of it, and red.
The blue vanishes.
The sun is faint,
suddenly hurricanic.

I beach the canoe.
Birds rise.
The canoe wavers at sapling anchor

strains for midstream
and lake, muskellunge
in cold water brake.

Beneath the marsh grass
routes for ferrets
tracks for snouts,
mouths feeding on veins,
capillary streams.

My boots are soaked past the laces.
I am in past my knees.

4.

Whish and *slash* of weed spear,
scrape and tear of lily pad,
scum on drowned spruce branches.

The prow rises.
The paddle drips fine silt.

Air, sharp diamond,
pricks my throat.
My shirt is soaked.
Pike weed
trails from my hand.

A mouth, gelatin hard
swirls and sinks.
A muskellunge strikes.
Water and a stone
mica-shining below.

I crave for a voice, for
my father, for a soldier,

a swimmer, for my dead cousin,
for John Dillinger.

5.

As the canoe fans,
turns upon a vitrescent wave
the color of cinnamon,
the sun blisters forth,
a tangle within a body,
within a chest.
The north sky then
slides with ice light in day light.
Clattering reeds and grasses.
A merganser honks, banks,
and strikes north.
A claw draws up a black lamp
towards Cassiopeia.

NIGHT SWIM

The wild apples were bitter, as we knew
they were. We skipped them
over the lake, quit finally and built
a fire on the shore. Three of us
crouched near the flames.
Toads swam to the firelight
from all over the lake.
On the oily surface, their knobby heads
left wakes. I reached along the sand
and touched Bill's scrotum.
I held him in my hand, as the toads hopped
from the black water, croaking,
tumbling over one another
in copulations, beside the fire.

EILEEN

1.

Meet me in the root cellar,
earth, a kerosene light,
burlap,
no thought of morning

to answer this
why without flowers
you overwhelm me
with orchids and violets

to the act
of my loving you
myself as rigid earth
lying without blankets
for hours in the musk
without caring

brought into it
into its treasure,
the pounding hooves of goats,
the red tongues of parrots.

2.

A mood disrupted the black fog
threw off singly the burlap bags.
Who could be natural?
The pickle jars sneering overhead
the stench of rotting potatoes
whiffed sensuality
fat wet mushrooms,
carrots, onions softening.

Nor did fantasy work.
It shrivelled when you said
"Don't be dirty."

I dropped free, dressed again
in my own clothing
but did not know it.

NUDE FATHER

I've never stopped, even in my sleep,
seeing him in the lake
facing me with his hands all wax
over his sex. His throat and wrists
are sun burned. He is so white.
He splashes me with water.

I yank my baggy swim trunks off,
dive, and reach cold mud.
I hold a submerged tree branch.

I surface as he retrieves his clothes.
He keeps on walking, nude,
entices me to follow, at the rear.

CARNIVAL MAN

I tried to lock the door.
The sound of whipped leaves was hard to bear.
I pounded my feet on the floor.
I should not have gone to the fair.

I had helped him erect the tent.
We both held the central pole.
He was Southern, brown, magnificent.
I was his branch, he was my bole.

I watched him undress in his trailer.
He thought I was older then.
He gave me two dollars for my labor,
and said "keep growing"—he'd be back again.

I couldn't lock the door.
Horses were loose in the storm.
I huddled on the floor.
I shouldn't have gone to the fair!

WHAT JOHN DILLINGER
MEANT TO ME

The Wisconsin lodge
where Dillinger slept
with Evelyn Frechette
in a musty bedroom
hung with stag horns
is legend, has become locale.

>   *Last week there were arbutus*
>   *this week violets,*
>   *and next there will be snow.*

Here was Robin Hood,
thirsting, despising law,
loner, who by miracle
knew and fled,
left Evelyn behind,
her and her friend.

>   *And snow follows snow.*
>   *Flickers drill the trunks*
>   *of evergreens for grubs and*
>   *nuts stored there by squirrels.*

>   *Bears lie fallow,*
>   *The paps of summer in their dreams.*
>   *Skunks garner oil,*
>   *rub their legs together*
>   *to quiet the seeping.*

I did not see the pustules
on his jaw, the chipped tooth
the crooked finger, the fact
that he had clap. His hands

were beautiful. His breath
as fragrant as one of Solomon's lovers.

And his picture
on my bedroom wall,
pasted to the corrugated box
smashed flat and nailed
to the two-by-fours
to keep out cold!
How immaculate his stance
before his flivver!
Felt hat back on his head,
shirt sleeves rolled
above the elbow,
trousers high on the waist,
a band, Hollywood style,
set with pearls to hold them tight.
His legs spread wide,
and, held even with his navel,
his Tommy gun. Again
the stance, a perfect V,
zodiac man.

What had gone wrong
at the forked bridge
outside the town? What
had transpired at Sunday School?
Was it poverty? Despair?
The wheel at the fair?

The gingerbread man
rides the stream
on the slick nose of the fox,
Robin Hood romps in a costume,
Arthur in armor.

NIGHT VISITOR

Night sweat, hard breathing.
Agate moonlight shed through the window,
as the outlaw, white-throated,
in a white shirt with rolled sleeves
strokes the sleeping boy's shoulder.

He lifts the boy and holds him
sheetless, nude.
The boy tastes Dillinger's mouth,
the fleshed inner lip, the tongue,
the zinc-taste of saliva.
"Take me!" the boy pleads.
The creaking is the roof's wind,
the bronze spittle of home.

SNOW IMAGE

I quarry his image from snow.
The radio says he has fled—
to Wisconsin or Illinois.

On the roof feet tread.
A man in a silver sky
wears holsters of stars.

He covers my eyes.
"Sleep," he says. "Sleep."
His face is on my pillow.

Blood drenches the clothes my mother dries.
Blood frosts her fresh baked cake.

DILLINGER IN WISCONSIN

1.

He drives north, 300 miles,
in his Hudson Terraplane.
"Leach, you fucker," he exclaims,
"I'll get you! Purvis, you scum,
kinky-haired Hoover's pretty boy,
Shove this up your ass!"

Then he misses Billie who is in jail.
They are already on his trail.

2.

J. Edgar Hoover flails the roadside
trees. The stench of an Illinois jail
on the night breeze. Shotgun barrels
protrude from white birch trees.
North of Oshkosh, fallow rolling fields.

Jiggling lights (a Model-A Ford) speeding.
Dillinger detours. The auto passes.
No guns or whistles in these pristine woods.

3.

He looks at who he was, before he dies—
if he should die. That damn gross penis!
Huge prepuce, stone. Even at fifteen
it wouldn't let him alone, clumped
between his legs, obscene,
in his overalls or gabardines:
big head, bemused,
nestling over the tight balls.

He hated the smegma in his clothes,
the stale wool, the pulpy skin
between his toes. He kept
to the far corners of the school.
Baths were once a week, as a rule,
in a galvanized tub near a kitchen stool.
His dad soaked his back,
or his sister Audrey might,
if her husband wasn't home that night,
off playing poker with the boys
or smooching at the picture show.

4.

He stops beside the road.
He climbs out, yawns and inhales
the piney air. The stony road
reflects moonlight in its ruts,
dark spruce and tamarack spires.
Blueberry swamp.
Two more hours to Little Bohemia.

He thinks of Billie in her bed.
He kisses her nipples.
He cradles her head, then
thinks of how she'd bled
when he first took her.
His loins are parched.
He rubs his glans with snow.
"Billie, Billie," he says.
His perineum burns.
Hot copper moves over his lips.
He strokes his groin, harder! harder!

EVERYWHERE, YET NOWHERE

1.

He escaped, remained as elusive as air.
He seemed to be everywhere, yet nowhere.

2.

"Well,
they had Dillinger
surrounded
and was
all ready to shoot him
when he came out,
but then
another bunch of folks
came out ahead,
so
they just shot them instead.
Dillinger
is going to acci-
dentally get with
some innocent by-
standers some time,
then
he will get shot."—Will Rogers

ON NOT ATTENDING MY FATHER'S FUNERAL

1.

The land was rock and sand,
the growing season short,
the acreage minute.
We hoed potatoes, watched
corn sprout, cultivated turnips
for the hogs to eat.
Dad was always there.

He barely wrote.
He almost never read.
His language, though,
bred similes and metaphors.
He taught himself to play six instruments.
He could fix anybody's car.
He swung farm implements
as if the earth loved his assault.
Even fatigued he laughed.
He often sang.
I could not bear his absences at work.

He built a house of timbers
he himself had hewn.
He added other rooms,
modified the roof hip-style,
and piled rock, stone-boated
from the field, for a basement.
He shot deer, rabbit, quail.
He hooked fish through the ice.
His labors were in pleasing us.
We rode to town with him
in a model-A sedan he'd converted to a truck.

He breathed in fumes welding in shipyards
and drank to counteract the smoke.
He never saw a doctor, lived on beer and soda.
Later, he bought a welding shop,
inhaled more fumes, cast seams
but never charged enough.
He reviled himself, lamenting
his dead brothers and sister,
aching for his mom.
He stopped singing, spent hours
before the television set.

He built a second house of cinder blocks.
Studs and two-by-fours
left bare, a primer coat of paint,
a pocked concrete floor.
He was always cold.
His cars ran, but now never
with that earlier precision.
He grew indifferent to his gift of touch.

A bone prodded him.
A cancer was excised.
He walked huddled in a soiled overcoat,
needing a cane.

2.

The town dump in mist and fog.
Girls brought a dog for him to shoot.
He placed the rifle to its skull,
pulled the trigger, and missed.
He fell in leafless brush, dead.

3.

I won't see him dead, flesh
pummeled into shape and life-colored
by a cosmetologist!

Speak, Dad! Sing!
The flesh I grasp—my own,
my sons', my lover's—
is your continuing life.
My fantasies are yours.
The animals you shot crouch on my path.
I stroke their fur, close their eyes.
Your fiddle and accordion waltz past.
Your metaphors whirl through my mind.

4.

I have not taken his picture from my shelf,
nor his poster from my wall.

I've had my own flames, breath to burn.
I believe the real Dillinger got away.

They shot the man without a mole, without a car.
There was a stand-in at the Biograph Theater.

MOTHER

1.

The resuscitation team had little time
for decency: his mother lay on the floor
with her nightie hiked around her neck.
The team seemed indifferent
to the shanks, the little body like a worm
in a nutshell, the sagging breasts.

He grabbed an afghan from the couch, one
full of flower-colors, and covered her parts.

The team kept thumping on her chest.
They clamped oxygen over her mouth.
Nothing helped, as she sank deeper
into the floor, through the cement slab,
lower than the potatoes.

2.

While the grave-digger
dug the grave
squirrels romped beneath an oak.

The old digger cut quilt-exact
squares of turf and piled them
on a tarmac. His shovel
cut easily through the roots and loam.

His mother would lie beside his dad,
her concrete box containing her blue
coffin touching his gray concrete box
containing his brown coffin.

He had the digger pause while he stroked
his dad's box: dead twelve years—bones,
shredded clothes, and little black beads
for his eyes. The sand was carrot-red.
Would their juices, in the sense of mush,
seep through to some neutral space?

His mother preferred no coffins or cement—
just her corpse arranged feet down, head up,
in the sand. He had touched her hands
and kissed her forehead and knew
how iced-over death is.

Spiney carrot tops struck him in the face,
hard across the mouth.

III: GARY

Sometimes with one I love I fill myself with rage for fear
   I effuse unreturn'd love,
But now I think there is no unreturn'd love....

—Walt Whitman

Cold stars
have said it all

and turbulence
dies, misfiring
meaning to kill you.

As rigid
as a naked archer
frozen through eons

blizzards (what
new creature will lap
up pools of fire?).

That we were one and
one. Whatever is creased
to make a fan, whatever

craves to dance, and can,
as I fall from you, as
you leave, mountains

of ice rise, vast peaks
of blue and white. Who
knows, how can I ever know?

Those barking monsters
and craters are
the frozen tongues of God.

I thought that to fall
was to know. I thought
that to know was to fall.

* * *

You turn
from the corner of the room
and face me.
Your eyes are calm.

I enter them
never leave
never have to sleep.

* * *

That line
running
from the soft hollow
of your throat, down
the chest to the navel
loses itself in hair.
I follow it with lips
and tongue
along its moist rib valley,
turning with it
onto your taut belly.
I draw your legs to my face,
bury there, withdraw.
My arms push full-length
down your sides
from hip to armpit,
push, press:
halves into a whole.
Fractured light exploding.

* * *

Your fists are warm
against my ribs.

The musk of love
is hot mercury
pressed between
layers of skin.

At last
cool zebras of light
are feeding.

* * *

A dead bird
this morning
in the back yard.
A wren by the chrysanthemum
its breast chewed open.
Cat or skunk ravenous
for heart and lungs.

Feathers stir in the wind.
A small tick (orange)
shivers and creeps
into the orifice,
into cold meat
and muscle.

I see you, love,
your brown eyes
open and still
lying on the green
surface of the moon
and I am eating your heart.

* * *

Night comes on.
We halt
on the walk
beside the lamp
before the lighted shop.
The sun has dropped.
You cannot see.

I lift your eyelid
scan for the lens
locate it
where fine hair begins
wonder
how to move it

to its place
without impacting
grain, soot, scratch
of diamond on
gelatinous glass.

Glass moves
rising, adhering now.
I touch eye water.

Night comes on.
It is the skin
that fails to let us in.

* * *

You stand sideways in the light.
I love your body,
have, shall and will.
I see everything as a wedge.
Tell me.
There's meat in the butcher shop window.

Pass from my life, now,
just as you came.
Let it rain.

* * *

My brain flashes
crystals of light,
no panic, no fright.
I have dug someone's grave
with my teeth.
Still twitching
he lies beside me on a beach.
I kiss him, bury him.
I do not even know his name
or why he came.

* * *

Your hints assume
the subtlety of elephants
crossing ice. I resist
until my own beasts rampage.
I divert their charge towards me
to you.

* * *

I've lost again.
The ape of love
swings on his vine.
I didn't mean for you to be
the victim, the hurt lip
salving the blister.

* * *

We found a continent:
lianas, spoor, and needle-vermin.
Bananas and milk
consumed beside the water.
Each morning was scarlet,
each night a superb closed rose.
I want to be clear:
there were nerves,
brimstone, gall.
But what a trumpeting,
what a rending
of throats and bellies,
fires in paradise!

That land is an isthmus now,
less than a cart track to home.
And the isthmus is burning.
Leaves of mold drop.
A one-eyed jackal with a black tongue

limps to a stream and pisses.
We are riven.

I want to grab an eagle eating its meat
and, eye to eye, mouth to beak,
crush it.

* * *

Sheer meat spits words
(the market hasn't closed)
revokes night, sun
and all the constellations.
I write this on a node,
not a rock.

* * *

Swinging through arbors,
vine past vine, elm after elm,
bodies burn. What letters
are you writing?
Are you cooling the wine
in the public fountain?

In the zoo
an ape shafts itself with a stick,
an elk is a monument,
a bear thrusts a mirror down its throat.
I bring today's mail.
No news to speak of.

And you are here
within the Lehmbruck statue
breathing clay, slim arms
and legs, hammered chest and groin,
feet waiting for the next need.
It comes down to skin,
impermeable tissue drawn tight
over the heads of selves

beautiful, trenchant, askew.

* * *

I know what drifting means.
Water, pellucid, gathers
where friction is applied.
A rich callous crusted
with tough flake skin
delays a final eruption.

Your hands
are so soft between the fingers
when touched and bitten.

You have to say
we are in lust
want to be had
blisters burned black
by fire-weed.

Draw your hand over my face.
I'll wait.

* * *

My mood tonight
howls blacks and reds.
I could fuck tables, chairs,
dishwashers, or owls.
The self won't do.
I observe my leg.
Nothing ascends.
My hand rests by a cup,
so calm. In my brain
parrots screw one another.

* * *

You are moving naked in sleep,
in your warm bed, in your room

(you need socks, a sweater, shoes).
You are coming to adore
wearing ripped things.

I walk, sleeping.
A bird drags itself through my heart.
I am cold.
In a few hours it will be morning.
This day will flash with a silver light.
Extend your hand, waking.
Touch me.

* * *

Each time you say
you feel like a virgin:
each nerve swollen
with blood and bitten
is ravished afresh,
the ripped cloth wound
over your loins lifts off, tightens,
ensnares you symbolically,
against your will,
loving it.
For me
each encounter
is a million hours old.
Perhaps that's why I'm anxious,
don't waste time pretending
we've just met in a tropical garden,
on monastery land.
I want to leap past gestures,
to savor cinnamon, eat crushed thyme
and fall, locked, with you
through to that kingdom
of exhaustion, wet
breathing nerve-and-sinew
wisdom, scorching the gods.

* * *

He fell through stars
through polluted air
to reach you sleeping.

You've wanted him to come
have kissed David's
ivory balls and wound
the figurine in silk,
in rituals of craving.

When he wakes you
and you turn over moist, warm,
surprised,
let him kiss you
let him rub his hot
celestial cock
against your groin,
let him drive it in,
as slick as steel, ravishing
and when he explodes
and floods your navel
know, love, that he'll
withdraw more easily
than he came, leave you
with the sound of his wings
beating out of the room
away from the castle,
on to other hungry dreamers.

I want to hold you.

* * *

The scissors work this time,
for the last time.
You've said you're not returning.
Something is rotten.
No intimacy or breath, it seems,

can draw meat back to health
fit to be eaten
(I think of you
screwing in the baths
and being screwed).
I won't drop to the floor
for crumbs, or wail
that you've left me burning
for the word that won't come,
to resolve us
for another week, month,
another year.

* * *

Everyone it seems complains.
But not now.
Can I keep on trusting you?

You bring me light—an odor
of plums, tin, and silver cooling.

Who was at the door?
Don't be angry again.
Why should I leave the bath?

You have scattered the brains of poems
over my pillow.

* * *

The bedrooms are deserted:
carpet lint, green sills,
dead wasps in the corners.
A ghost just shut an attic door
and went outside.
Nothing doing in here:
there's a fire, a candle,
blankets thrown back,

window ajar for air.
You say you're tired.
A creosote timber.
My eyes won't shut.
Strained nuclei shift
from and into sleep
charging ions of need, teeth.
My pastures quake
with bulls humping cows.

* * *

There is this end for the night:
it will be there pulverizing bones,
beating water into silt,
or, it shall ride like black dawn
meeting itself east, over the sea.
We feel its breath and, like it,
draw closer into a doubled morning rose.

IV: MARRIAGE

This is the maiden all forlorn, a
      crumpled cow with a crumpled horn
Who lived in the house that Jack built.
This is the crab-god shiny and bright
      who sunned by day and wrote by night
      and lived in the house that Jack built.

—Jack Spicer

SEPARATION POEM

The tide
crests and crumbles white brain matter.
Love's jewels are bloody, drenched,
tarnished by light, sputum, and gall.
Dragging its leg
the world wails for a doctor.

ON BEING AWAKENED TOO EARLY
AFTER A NIGHT OF ARGUMENT

Sarcasm along a nerve.
I fight for calm.
Where will this argument lead?
In the end, in bed, we shall screw.
But, in the morning
when the garbage truck clanks by
and the badly adjusted sprinklers
lash water against the door
we shall wake, early,
before hate
sliced into our marrow
has dissolved sleep,
fading as cortisone
through a vein.

SO FAR, FEW WOLF CHILDREN
HAVE BEEN AUTHENTICATED

I walk all night along the street
craving
to expose the dime
burning my pocket.

Adorned white horses prance,
jingle bridle bells,
raise hooves, eyes
sapphire bright.

What to do
when ratiocination
swallows its own stinking breath,
frog-gutted, tummied,
waits to feel a straw
shoved up its ass,
threatens to burst
unless additional
pressure is produced.

If my hair were gray and longer,
if my will were stronger
and I had no debts...

It is the wolf,
keen moon howler,
that we seek,
and a stance in a field of stones,
and rain, drizzling sleet, hail
and at last a cave of guano
the debris coughed up by owls
(sweet small deer devoured),
a nest of leaves,

and a she wolf braced
on all fours, pumice-toned,
udder exposed, nipples erect
at right angles,
to be sucked, gummed
by desperate ones.

Dreams
fall out of the nest
of chaste moments.
Slate-colored proprieties
at last
       drown
as the mouth
dribbles   runs with
fresh white wolf milk.

ON CUTTING

A great heave of breath
whets the knife.

NUDE FATHER WITH
SLEEPING SON

White shoulder
   at a three-quarter turn.
He can't discern his son's face.
   Above the armpit
vulnerable magenta on white.
   Lymphatic waters.
He cradles his son: soft cartilage,
   night-wet curls,
velvet patella, neck-rift,
   warm shoulder depression.
There is glue near his eye.
   The ball of his abdomen is bloody.
Green on his buttocks.
   Treacle flows down his skull
smothering his jugular.

He thinks: *marble, onyx,*
   blue nostrils clogged with cotton,
   vertebrae detached.

He returns the boy to bed.
   He waits near the window,
sweeps his arm towards a star
   but is pricked,
fears anguish,
   doesn't know where to fling his arms.

SEURAT

A boy in a red hat and red trunks
stands waist-deep in a river,
his hands to his mouth, calling.
His back, immense lung space,
is hunched with power.
Tied with ribbons
his voice floats over the water,
bands of pure color,
silk and rayon, sexual.

DEPARTURE POEM

There's little
to show
you were here: a
sock, trousers, a book
half-read, the
rattan chair you
liked, the bed
you escaped to
when I wanted in.
Why stay here
in the same town?

Flower lint
drifts past my face.
Strips of skin drift.
My brain drips
red berry clusters
Gather them! Gather them!

SON

1.

You've begun to feel
how skin creeps, how blisters start
when leather pinches the heart.
Caught in my own ice
I've not found time to pitch a ball
or swing you through the parlor.
I've loved you
drenched in a brown light
shed from my mind (who loses
the real also drops the false).

2.

I stand by your bed.
A harsh wind beats bamboo
outside the window.
Your stuffed lion roars.
Someday the earth will boil
purple, raging, and die.
Please, waste laughter.
Ravish each day.
Forgive me for going away.

ON WALKING NUDE IN THE
SAN BERNARDINO MOUNTAINS

1.

Gray shale over the trail.
A fallen redwood tree.
A branch snaps. Flowers and sparrows.
Mist and snow. Chickadees.
I am metal inside metal.

2.

Says a philosopher: who lives
in a house with himself
must invent his talk
or do without.
There is, of course,
the possibility of a drought.

3.

My family visit a meadow.
A picnic on the grass.
My sons fish in a stream. My wife
serves strawberries and whipped cream.
My daughter sketches a magic flower
carried by a mouse to its mouse-
lover's bower.
My wife looks up, crying.
My younger son starts whining.
My daughter flings her drawing
into the stream. My other son
breaks his fishing rod on a boulder.
I couldn't get to them if I tried.
It wouldn't comfort them if I cried.
I couldn't help them if I died.

ON DEFINING POSITIONS

A Chinese elm
surrounded by ivy
itself contained by
brick and a picket fence
overlooking the sea.
Who owns the tree?

Since you raise the question
I turn that way.
It has to do with loving,
and why once near the beach
I always scurry home.

I want to go East, you say,
looking up at the sun.
(Whose tree? Whose sun?)
Something attends a burial.
Nothing replaces itself.

CAUGHT

That branch
displays
toes in motion,
moving towards a stone:
the knee
of the left twigfork
bends
to accommodate
a cone.
the right fork
nervous to proceed
sheds bark.

LOVE POEM

We should not have gone.
I should have expected crows
not swans to keep the time.
Observe the ice in the glass,
a clock hand embedded in a green shoulder.

Your intensity glows
with the after-hue of a burner
freshly extinguished.
My gaucheries hiss
as water drops bounce and roll,
hiss bounce and roll.

Douse the light.
Lie silent—the whisker
of a rat—beside me.
A taste of zinc persists.
The hours have wrenched
the sprocket from the chain.

EASTER POEM

Your yard flood light goes on.
The stone fountain plaster child.
A hose spurting water.
I don't know where you are,
at which bar. I think
of Easter, and what you said
of love and lovers,
and I don't know
whose need is greater,
or if we can find what we're after.

ROCKING CHAIRS
ON THE BEACH

The beach
is full of them today
tubular aluminum frames
and plastic webbing rockers in rows.

Laughing, mothers wipe grit
from their eyes. Musclemen
ride trapezes midair and fall.
Children run away.
Automobiles reverse themselves.

O, chairs,
rocking to the water,
will there be sweet gurgling
when the waves roll over you,
and you go under screaming?

You draw us into positions.
We squat in neat rows.
Our feet are under water.

AT LAST, SOMETHING IS IN SEASON

A weathered plank with seven bent rusted nails,
blackberry brambles with fruit no larger
than the diamond in your ring.
Vines drop from a white pine.
Wasps spin like humming birds along
the pink slashed mouth of divorce.

This morning, on the trail, I came,
saying your name.

NOT TO SMILE IS TO COUNTERFEIT
THE URN-THING

This is your house, you've
said it. Yet you hate it.
This is your bed, true,
but the mattress is dying.

We laughed once
(there's a purple sex-lake near,
and thistles).
I hear what we meant still being spoken,
a scabbed throat choking out
scissors!

THE ESTRANGEMENT

You were so quiet at the place,
an hour before had said things
beyond backtracking—
testament for us both
as keen as a vein slashed open.

Was it the wild drive
along the ocean side,
the breakers to the right
and the red tide gleaming?
"We throw light onto the beach
down here," you said.

Clearly, being older
I had slammed the wrong gear.
Was tenderness lacking?
Scabrous throat channel of a mocking bird.
Birds swung in red bushes
outside the porch window.
I heard them all night.

And, yet,
at such times, it seems,
desire is at its whitest heat,
the jab of nerves transcended
as bells swing through the brain.
Guilt plugs my nostrils,
holes jabbed into cartilage,
as I rock in a chair at 4 a.m.
tied in, intent on walking out.

I GUESS YOU WON'T WANT THIS GIFT

Slap my face again
you say, at least

I'll know something
you mean, where I stand.

Why can't you come?
I have

and I have allowed you
a choice of
fingers, lips, glans.

Why was it
with someone else?

A fantasy jack frost
on a branch of icles.

TOPSOIL AND GREASE

Your children
lie in dried leaves.

They dropped from you torn.
That's how we're born.

ON CLIMBING A MOUNTAIN
WITH A SON

1.

Mercury adheres to a wire, in beads.
A cold fire, dusty sage, thistles.
We are drowning
or merely keeping abreast.

2.

A rock glistens with mica,
Jeff's finger on a world.
He leaps from stone to stone.
Snakes. Thistles rattle.
There is no floating.
My footprint covers his.
In the branches strands of yellow wool.

3.

I do not want his neck pierced
with cord and nail!
That trough at his throat
maintains his skull erect—
veins, striated marble, blue
over his temples.

4.

I break a branch.
It flames. The pad
of my hand burns.
A ram snared in a thicket.

5.

His hand
is made of wren's bones.
There is fear in his mouth.

PLEASE, DO NOT PUT ME ON

Begging is in style.
I've seen your lips turn blue
and trickle for money.
Feelings belie the truth:
who has hurt you, say it,
convulsively. Start with
a throatier pitch, always
eat your fingers and dimes.
No, don't piss here. Take
my wallet. Watch how
this parrot eats sunflower
seed: his tongue
blunders over his beak.
He says *money, money.*
What a way to wander.
What a way to say I love you.

ON COMMITTING ADULTERY
FOR THE FIRST TIME

A *spink* of water
drips from the
cabin shower head.

I can't turn it off.
Spink. Spink.
All through the night.

The time for perfection
is not ripe, my dear,
for more than rutting

after the spotted chestnuts
of each day's foraging.
We can't do better.
The fault's mine.

I'll wind grape leaves
in my hair, pretend...
But nothing happens.

Spink. Spink. Spink.
I try to swing outside my brain,
but can't.

WHY DON'T THEY GO BACK
TO TRANSYLVANIA?

Gulping air, two of them
grip my shoulders.
There are little white clits
in their mouths.

They beat me.
I grab one and pull.
Its teeth clamp shut.
Its claws bunch like fists.
I sear them with matches.
The rat back humps and squeals.
Blood spatters my shoulders.

They have me pegged for the wrong mania.
Why can't they go back to Transylvania?

PINK WINDOW

For days you walk through a pink window. It's mullioned.
You found it hanging from a tree in the woods.
Where is the old woman's house?

The window falls to the ground. You take it, certain
you'll never reach home. You stick to the window.
Your hands glue to its sides. The window laughs. It
directs you up this trail, down that one. Cobwebs
form over its ogeed point.

WHY ARE YOU LATE
IN COMING HOME?

I found your farewell notes
all in blue ink, on a page.
I took them up, put them down,
and took them up again.
And now you are late.
Under this flagrant sun
I want to know what's done.
Have you flung yourself
at a freeway guard rail?
An ambulance races towards
San Bernardino.
Are you over a cliff?
Is Judas in a tree?
Is it me?
My night is rigged with meteors.
Each waking hour moves on toes, bare,
along a mile-high electric wire.

THE SUN IS IN THE TREES

Green shapes, shaking from
dark to light, in a fractured mind.
Scraps of skin.
Bits of liver, speckled old chocolate.
Tallow-strip memories
of when we were needed.
Decay
burns us away.

EPITAPH

He lost his mind
pursuing boys in leather jackets
and girls in boots.
He had begun to puff out at age 30,
to lose roots, so to speak,
in his normal scene.
He forgot to shave,
drank his liquor rough,
turned from fiction to verse,
and had success.
He kept the ugliest pigeons
he could find for pets.
Now he is seaweed,
now he is salt.
Motorcycles scream
past his ebbing place,
riding further out on every tide.
Girls descend,
wiggle and squirm to disco rock,
and when they remember him
they do so with a grin
untouched by the pustulence
he left in his works.
Inside a chromosome
pink devils persecute angels:
pitchforks rip throats,
fangs bite in places for navels.
Harps and lyres smash, quiver,
and incinerate. Golden apples
fall, mangled by red beetles.
Fart sounds and belching.

THE DROWNED MAN
TO THE FISH

Fish,
a line of gut
connects you to me.
Fish,
your belly
is as taut and green as mine.
Flesh under your tail
has drawn away—bleached vertebrae.
My backbone jells.

Your mouth mirrors mine.
My lips are cartilage.
My teeth are falling,
water soaks the roots.
My tongue is a spoon.

We drift:
little variation
in the fathoms we are down.
We approach the Bahamas, I think,
or Florida, or Bimini, or a Key.
Draw closer to me.
I am neither warm nor cold,
am softening,
am bloated and old.

How did you drown?
Head down, tail up?
I drowned standing
where I fell, planted.
What was it you wanted?
A better world?

Finless and armless we float.
One finger rubs the flesh off another,
a fin flapped by a current
drops scum and scales.
We shall be final bone,
following head to pelvis,
to limbs, to spine,
a design.

V: PAUL

Our nerves ecstatically bite
pain away. Rings around our bodies
swirl like Saturn's.

—Paul Trachtenberg

GOODNIGHT, PAUL

In "Goodnight, Paul" Constance Talmadge
arranges her peach-toned negligee
so that the sparrow breast throb of her pulse
winks chiffon and seduces Edmund Lowe
before the night and the wine sour.
She's a vamp. She loves the script.
Her tight blonde curls prick her cheeks.
She wears a rhinestone clip and stiletto heels.
Will Lowe have taped his foreskin,
nestling the excess in cellophane?
Raising her glass she squeals.
A lipstick flash. The tip of her tongue
is a little hatless man in a boat.

Each night, thumbtacked to your door,
her poster, smiling, tucked you in.
The mint on your teeth, your body in the sheets,
the whoosh of rain, the carp pond flashing fins.
On your move to another town,
you junked the poster, and, now
there are no copies, at any price.

Though vaporous, Talmadge remains,
yes, raising her long-stemmed glass,
clicking her heels, caressing her silky haunch:
"Good night, Paul."

Note: The film "Good Night, Paul," a silent five-reeler,
directed by Walter Edwards, was released in 1918. It was
based on a successful stage play with book and lyrics by Roland
Oliver and Charles Dickson, and with music by Harry Olsen.

IN THE PARK

Jump. Thrust your legs over the bar
holding the gym rings in Kiddies' Park.
Grab two more rings and angle downward.
Turn your face this way, smiling.
Now, hit the sandpile!

There's no false armor here,
no supermarket dross, poisoned apples,
disgrace notes, ravished damsels, pennants
from lost wars, no snivelling Lancelot.
Hollow licorice stems secure this kingdom.
Swing, spin the world on its head,
kick the traces. Laugh like a prince.

THE SKINTLED GARDEN WALL

The essentials: trowel, cement mix,
oil pan, brick. The plumb line follows
the grain until the wall curves up
in a high baroque, non-American twist.

No more termite-riddled wood,
apostrophes of plank eaten paper-thin,
syllables of weeds, thirsting
honeysuckle verbs and passion vines.

LEAF HOPPER

Was it a miracle
the gross leaf hopper?

You beheaded him with a trimmer:
the mandibles kept twitching
in the redwood chips.
The body spun in a frenzy,
ramming a window sill.
He swept past your shoe,
wiped his legs fastidiously
and died.

THERE'S PAIN IN GARDENING, AS THERE IS IN POETRY

Those aphids sucking your whorled
rose buds and stems, the mildewed leaves,
the bronzed petals, the rust-sifts
resembling burnt cicada shells,
the enormous green hopper chomping
vertiginous paths through the leaves.
These could drive one from floriculture
to weaving tapestries.

You apply dust, jet-spray poison,
rive the hopper, feed the bushes sulphate,
zinc, crushed oyster shells.
Yet, O rose you are sick!

ON THE BEACH

Near dawn, a shrieking sea gull
is a cello scraping tunes
in an old folks' home.
Nary a dog stirs. The tide persists.
Yellow pier light is phosphorescent.
Oil rigs glisten.

When I left the house for the jetty
you were asleep.

A dead seal: an open mouth as a white heart,
pink froth, a gunshot wound.
I circle him then proceed south.
Exhilaration, yes.
Salmon clouds. Morning. Rain.
Loving you.

TORSO

His nipples resemble apricots.
His biceps are sheathed,
forearm turned palm up, vulnerable,
sinew attached to bone, etcetera.

By not flirting, the glissando of his speech
rang both with sex and the nature of God.

You crave his image, waft him
through wood smoke, distress, and jagged glass.

BLUE EGGS ON MY TABLE

Birds in yolk, albumin, and water.
No warmth in a chilled house.

One egg loves
a plaster Mexican Jesus.
Blood bathes the gem.
The foetus quickens.

Egg two is yours,
tumescent, spent, addled, flayed.
Your semen shoots
and no one takes it.

Egg three is a fire.
Tie it to your throat.

In a cypress tree
parrots scream.

What's lost may never be found.
What's found will be lost forever.

A TENSILE METAPHOR

Rouse those lovers before they're crushed.
Yes, I know, they suck and pump
oblivious to fate's raunchy snap.
Don't feel too sorry:
love is always better
on a mattress in the street.
There's no time to explain.

GARY

He kept himself dangling from the telephone.
He would retrieve the missing cufflinks
tying him to what was tender.
He tossed his head back
as blood gushed over his teeth.
For he had lied.
The next morning he climbed a mountain,
shot himself, died, and was retrieved
by Air Force men from the nearby base.
He should have fought back, you said,
since he was so exorcised. You pointed
towards the schist where he crashed.
He'd always craved death, something
about an uncle who willed him a watch.
Moreover, it's easy not to fight,
dancing to Grandma's house.
He loved the greasy base ball bat
thrust up his ass by the photographer.
He ate mustard, stoned,
and had his cock ridiculed in that porn flick,
as *Michael Tremor*, a sick joke.
Life, he said, isn't always Cracker Jack.
He grins from a eucalyptus tree.
"We remember you," I say.
He rejoins the shades.
A naked snapping in the mist,
a jiggling in a palm, high up
where spidery hairs inseminate dates.

CHRISTMAS

1.

The tree strung with red apples,
snowflakes, the flickering lights,
the shopping trips,
the mediocre films—each one
the spent carcass of a partridge
shot from its pear tree,
Godiva chocolates,
trips through the neighborhood,
electronic life-sized teddy bears,
gingerbread, multi-colored house-wrap
whipped off the nails by winds,
light-pole candy canes, the "Chipmunks"
retailing their carols,
ersatz icicles, the old tin Coca Cola
Santa positioned near the weepy image
of wise men lascivious for Mary's nipples,
Joseph amazed.
Much rime in the California light
sparkles on all the dichondra lawns at night.

2.

My Wisconsin boyhood:
wind whirling updrafts through the tin
stove pipe, thrumming the guy wires,
the orange, the apple, the ribbon candy,
the bland coloring books, the wool socks,
the tree fetched from the woods, on skis.

3.

Here, in California, the season
is whisker-brushed by mice nibbling

frankincense. Shampooed dogs
dream of basset hound Saint Nicks
loaded with Kibbles and Gravy Train.
Chiffon snow sifts the roof.
At 2 a.m. the prancing of hooves
and a mighty *ho ho ho*.

NEARLY MORNING

My flannel comforter
is as warm as yours.
(Are you sleeping on your side?)
True, hands warm genitals,
as does the sun, or fire.

In my dream a stubby man
grinds a knife against his jugular,
spews forth neither blood nor rage,
though the slice is keen.
He was in a deep stone well
and drew himself to the lip.
I hear his cry.
Ivy sprang from his fingers.
"No!" I shout.

GRANDMA

Rage overpowers her homespun skirts, her plaited hair.
She's lost a screw for a bamboo window blind.
She wants to trench zinnias
but can't find a spade. And where
are the keys for the Dodge
and the silver urn for tears
(memento of Margaret Dumont,
dowager of the Marx Brothers movies)?
Huddled on a braided rug, Granny convulses.

She stops sobbing. She rises. There's
the urn dumped of the heart ashes
of Dumont's favorite chihuahua!
She finds the key and the spade.
"Thank God," she exclaims, jerking a hair
from her nose. Then, on to the kitchen
where butter is softening—chocolate chip
cookies for her grandson Paul.

MAD KING LUDWIG

You perfume Cosa Rara, the King's white stallion
whose withers excite him to a fervor.
You own a gingerbread house lavish
with honey-colored balcony,
geraniums, gentians, and sweet Alpine air:
gifts of the monarch.

Your King meanders through a village,
burnt candle in hand,
his lederhosen open.
The air reeks with wood smoke.
Snow-laden spruce branches flare
with blood-black edges.

His underpants are grimed.
Scour them.
Yes, and his foul lust-cloths.
You whiff his black teeth
crammed as they are with rancid venison.
You are his man.

BAVARIA NEEDS HIM

The King's robe
frays at the neck—the effect
is of a purple hound riddled with mange.
He trips over his gold caftan
which sags over his paunch,
and, with scissors in hand,
in dim candle light, inspects the robe,
then orders a throne
from which he lambastes an architect
for creating arabesques, *not* Gothic pillars.
He dismisses his cousin Sophie
from his betrothal chamber
and seduces a groom.

Your threads stitch his public self
back into place. He must not
batter himself on the scenery
or collapse like a fat trout
in the middle of a speech
delivered with opprobrium and disgust.
He recites lines extolling
the naked loins of his soldier lover.
Bavaria needs him, you say,
as does Richard Wagner, as do we.

THE FATIGUED KING

1.

The king fatigued
props himself against the inner wall
of a bulbous Moorish tin kiosk
where he has sapped himself groping soldiers.
The soiled depressions
in the obese Turkish pillows dismay him.
For he repels the men.
When his mustache brushes a buttock
or his jewelled hand hefts a scrotum
the men swirl as if his sucking
were a joy. After all, these peasants
long ago threw off swaddling clothes.

2.

Below, in the stage pit
where the espresso percolates
and the bean sprout salads are served,
a red stereo system glows.
You look up, script in hand,
as I shout swan death songs,
then rip off my black wig.
My eyes are Ludwig's. And, yes,
the actor, too, fears death's stench,
as does the author,
as does the King.

NELL

Roisterous, strapping Nell
in her recycling center
in below zero weather,
a slippery over-hang of snow,
six-foot icicles.
Her space heater puffs, toasting her feet.
Her chair lacks slats.
Mice scurry behind the cardboard partition
and the cavernous bins of green and brown bottles
in freight car loads.
Flattened aluminum cans.
An acre of glass and metal.
"It's a living," she says.

The owner, in Michigan,
dumps the scrap-filled semis onto a barge.
He never pays the promised wage.
Nell threatens to burn the warehouse down.
"I'm like Dad," she boasts. "He sorted junk, too."

She wears Dad's old plaid coat.
She recites his jokes, wears gum boots,
carries a sheathed hunting knife,
pins topless calendar girls
among the invoices, cubic weights.
She whips most of the VFW at pool.
She's the only woman in America
to command a Legion post.
"You're something else, Paul," she says.
"Glad brother Bob brought you along.
Take a seat."

ENRAGED WOMAN

The woman obsessed with jigsaw puzzles
crammed the washer with Nell's clothes,
threw in a gallon of paint,
set the machine whirring,
slashed a floral living room couch,
wrote she was driving back to Missoula.

Earlier, on our Thanksgiving visit
Frieda wouldn't talk, either
because she'd been a nurse,
or was despised as a lesbian drunk.

She'd wheeled in furniture and clothes,
intending to stay forever, so she averred.
She failed to tell my sister of her cancer,
and that she hated sex.

My job was to roast venison,
hers to furnish tomato sauce, onions, cheese, and beans.
She had tight tallow-colored curls and razor lips.
She would pour salt down your throat.
She fiddled her own tunes.

Normally, we'd have stayed in Nell's house.
We rented a rustic motel.
It snowed the morning we left.
We imagined Frieda's boots
circling the car, casting charms.
A ten-pronged buck was foraging grasses:
pristine snowy forest vibrations
(where I was born), deliquescent speech,
a tamarack copse, skittering chickadees.
We've not been back.

A SENSIBLE OBSERVATION, A SENSIBLE QUESTION

Let's, I say, devour
smoked calamari
broiled with Danish ham.

A gray lighthouse blinks
as a purple dolphin careens
through a lurid sexual stream.

What a storm! Wet funeral chrysanthemums
bob and toss. I fear
a plumed cortege of outraged sea horses.

"A fine sense of fun,"
says a witch sporting a gardenia.
"Your body's camber tells me that.
So does your bitten tongue.

"You need an intellectual slave—
a tenor, bass, or a boy soprano.
You know the kind I mean.
Don't marry another poet."

I wave her off.
Obviously, as Jack Spicer wrote,
the grail is mine, obviously.

VI: NEW AND OLD

*A shriek ran thro' Eternity
And a paralytic stroke,
At the birth of the Human shadow.*

—William Blake

LINES ON AN ENGLISH
BUTCHER SHOP WINDOW
Christmas Poem 1966

O beautiful severed head of hog
O skewered lamb throat, marble eye
   of duck
O meadow freshened hare suspended
O lovely unplucked pheasant
   ripening in the gloom
O gracious suckling pig upended
O twisted tail erect
   and pinkish gouged-out hole
O graceful nub of sow tit, merry xylophone
   of fractured ribs
O rid ends smarting where the saw
   has severed you
O pleasant rind of fat and rosy spume
   along the incision sliced
   from genitals to snout
O livers tumbling, O clattering
   jewel of pancreas and ligaments
   of stomach wall
O golden brains emplattered
O calf-groin hacked in two
O carcass spiked, with legs
   encased and tied about
   with paper, hanging on the wall
O sheep form, severed shoulders,
O ham string of ox, O whitening lyre,
O steer loin pierced, O haunch,
O rib cage disembowelled
O glorious trays and juices, heaps of
   lamb hearts, chicken livers,
   gizzards, claws
I see you all!

FOR JEFF

I look at my daughter
and think she should have a piano.

—Greg Kuzma, "Piano"

My son should have his own camel,
one no higher than his waist.
It should have tufts of hair on its hump
and on its tail
with hairs on its lower jaw, its stupid
watery eyes, and navel.
Let it be painted like a zebra
or planted with a wig like a lion's.
Let Jeff confront the camel as it nibbles
my cabbages, and thrust it
by its tawny haunches and forelegs
over his head: a triumph over distractions—
the wish to do everything right,
to master French and Japanese.
At lunch, what a contentment,
sliced tomatoes, fish wrapped in kelp,
squid marinated in an inky sauce,
white rice, chopsticks,
and chocolate macadamia nuts.

I see Jeff at age six, when I left home
in cross-fires of emotion.
I see him at eleven climbing adobe villages
in Bandelier Park.
I watch him chin himself on a basketball net,
his ankles wrapped for outrageous jumps.
I love his powerful hands.
I love his laughter

as I struggle to be less demanding.
The summer, firm-toothed camel, slobbers
over sugared hay, twitching his tail,
expecting what he receives,
in whatever hues or intensities.

THE CHILD IN THE BURNT HOUSE

The child runs
through the burnt house.

He finds his father
charred, dead, huddled
under the stars.
He recognizes the face
and kisses it. His
father's hand falls off.
The child, with the hand,
climbs to the burnt roof.
The stairs come close.
They tell the child to sing,
but he can't do anything.

BRUEGHEL'S PIG

The world runs
with a knife struck through its hide,
a wedge sliced from its back.

THANKSGIVING DAY, 1989

My mother waits for me under a eucalyptus
in a barrio park in Santa Ana
for a free turkey dinner.
She's dissolved her halo, converted
her flowing gauze, Heaven-gown
to a day-glo pants suit
and has clamped her teeth back in.

"Being a ghost," she says, "and hence
lacking electrified synapses
I can stab my old face
with fork tines and not feel a thing.
My instep never itches
and my arteries are no longer clogged
with globular, rock-hard bacon fat.
I'm better off now—
although you're only three years
younger than I was when I died,
and you've already lived two years more than Pa.
I would not have returned, but
I saw you weren't invited anywhere
for dinner. None of your kids
is coming, and your friend Paul
is attending a dying uncle.
He'll wipe dressing across his lips
and whiff the steaming meat.
I don't mean to be crude, son."

"This is no laughing matter, I say.
"If you'd only warned me of your visit."

I found her at 5 a.m. on our porch
when I retrieved the L. A. *Times*.
She was smoking a cigarette,

waiting for the sun to rise
and for hummingbirds to sip dew
from my roses.

"I'd have made a fruit cake," I said,
"stuffed a goose with chestnuts,
whipped up your favorite pie—
pumpkin or pecan, both concocted
from Eagle Brand milk and brown sugar."

Going to the barrio seemed the best solution,
although she demurred: "Won't those brown
folk resent us?" On a rare visit I'd driven
her to Tia Juana to observe the indigents
colorized by merchants for enticing
gringo shoppers. She'd never
forgotten a small girl without panties
who squatted near her fruit-selling mother,
hiked up her skirts and urinated blood.
I'd dropped two quarters in the girl's palm
without ever touching her skin.
"Our poverty in Wisconsin was never this bad,
We always, as dad claimed,
had the proverbial pot to piss in."

White ladies and young bearded men
fetch turkey, dressing, cranberries,
peas, celery, carrot sticks, and yams.
The servers pose behind folding tables
covered with cheap turkey-motif paper.
Tripartite paper plates keep the cranberries
from floating through the peas.
A tape deck sizzles Christmas music
performed by "The Chipmunks."
The families get in line—we go to the rear.
Most fathers wear jeans.
Mothers wear bright head scarves.

"Look," mom observes, "the broader their asses,
the tighter the pants." Girls wear frilly
communion dresses. Boys sport casual clothes.
Assorted destitute whites. Emaciated
old bearded men in smelly trousers.
Dogs race under the tables.

Mom masticates her dinner with eclat, though
she does complain about the pies, deeming them
the sort churned forth by cheap supermarket
bakeries. The crust, which she leaves on her plate,
resembles wet sea sand. But she loves the pecans
in their butterscotch sauce
and stuffs a slab of turkey breast with same.
I can tell she's a ghost,
for the food floats off the fork
into her toothless mouth—no chewing,
no gullet gymnastics.

Later, I follow her to a slimy pond
befouled by coveys of slithering wood ducks.
"They're as obnoxious as snails," mom says.
"You can't eat 'em, and the conservationists
won't let boys torture and kill 'em. Look,
they keep those lovely mallards away."
She flings bits of potato, meat, and pie
to the latter. I'm nervous, for signs
forbid feeding the water-fowl, a misdemeanor.

Late afternoon. The fog is rolling in
though we are three miles from the beach. Mom
shivers. "I wasn't dressed for this."
I take her hand. "I'd like to see the ocean son.
I may not come again."
She's reassumes mystical attire.

We drive to the storm-damaged municipal pier.

She exits the car. "Wait, mom."
My voice is so subdued
I feel reverberations rather than hear them
"It's time," she says, kissing my forehead.
I let her hands drop. "A good day, son."
I say how much I've missed her.
A wheeling cloud suggests Beethoven's cranium.
Then, there's an art deco gourmet restaurant.
Misty angel figures raise gold goblets.
What are they singing?
"Mom! Mom!"

THE MAN WHO PLANTED A POTATO VINE IN HIS NAVEL

Some said it was
a miraculous potato-tree-of-Life.

Others said he was an asshole
and should cover the vine with a shirt.

"God's been good to me,"
he informed the editor
of the local paper.
"My vine blooms this week."

ESKIMO HAIKU

Drip. Drip. Drip.
Spring has come to my living room!

THE MURDERER

1.

A silicon brain—
or was it of onyx so hard
only diamond could scratch it?
Messianic: gold told him
to slaughter his family
then the rest of the world.
Finally, he would slash his own throat
and waft to Heaven and be God:
whoople cushions on His celestial throne,
leopards secured by jewelled thongs.
One of his ears was warmer
than the other. He'd trimmed
his beard so that his teeth glimmered vulpine
and yet, at the same time,
he was a perfect WASP.

2.

On the evening news his lower lip,
wet with glue, threatened to drip.
Half of his face wept,
the other half laughed.
Gargantuan dead eyes,
monosyllabic responses,
stupid on the President
of the country and the Congress.
A younger son had helped him
throttle an older son,
and in other murders.
How to get close to dad?
Play death-ball, go on Satanic
hunting trips, make man-talk.

ELDERLY DYING *AIDS* VICTIM

A man with croup, pneumonia, and bed sores
cuts strings of boy dolls from newspaper,
variously colored.

The boys chant: "We can't any more.
We won't come."

He's trapped inside a urine jug.
The sky glimmers through a magenta window.
A peach-toned hibiscus expires.
Snapping sounds, as though the petals (bacon)
are sizzling.

Flat on his back (those heinous carcinomas)
he beats time on the silly paper boys
dispersed over his chest.

A dirge evokes dragonfly wings clapping,
a hint of the Berlioz (or Verdi) *Requiem*.

He sees a bronze wall (Ashurbanipal's):
boys as gilt angels assemble
along a glowing coppery fissure.
Into this he slips, without bread,
without a sigh, into death's meal.

THE PHILOSOPHER

He's an old man,
an old philosopher.
He dies.
We embalm him
and wrap him in flannel.
We put him outside
on a wooden platform
near a limpid river channel.

He's dead for hours
among the hydrangeas, castor beans,
and other commemorating flowers.
We read his works.
They're full of quirks: too
Kantian, too Platonic, too erotic.
We laugh, go crazy, get it on,
an orgy. The wind
plays with his dead hair.
We show his dead eyes
pictures of Schopenhauer.

He stirs and yawns.
Slowly, he undoes his bonds.
He leaves his ankles tied.
He looks a little dried
from the formaldehyde.
He resembles Freud.
Like Socrates he sits
among his acolytes.
One leg dangles over his bed.
"Talk, talk, talk," he says,
"and fuck. That's all you do,
that's all you care about."

"Right on," we shout, wondering
what the miracle is all about.

He throws off his clothes.
He fingers his groin. His cock
rises like Lazarus from the grave.
He doesn't miss a stroke.
We chant in rhythm with his beat.
He dies and lies back down.
Angels the size of fireflies
materialize from his sperm.
Each angel's face
is a famous philosopher.

The angels flutter in a ring.
They clap their hands and sing.
They drop their angel clothes
and enter the old man's body.
He flies to the sky.

GORDON AT KHARTOUM

He watched the she-goat, glimpsed
her nubbed and ocher horns, her
low-slung womb, her nipples laden,
thrust against her awkward legs.
She would not make the hill.
The cracking fire would bring her down.
Her unborn young in the ripe
swimming sack would never know
that shock. Death would drown them,
a slow gurgling of wine death-water.

A chill sped through the palace.

It was noon. The white sun clung
to the Sudanese earth.
A fringe of color where the powdered
sky merged with the earth-heat
marked the enemy: spots of black boil,
lava spots under the glaring day.

He took the glass from the desk
and held it up: a one-humped
camel, legs apart, tail high,
urinating in the sand. He brought
the glass away. How silent in the palace!
The distant guns.

The goat stopped beside the gate
where no one was and pressed her
mouth against her side. How many young
she might have birthed! And milk
for the doomed, the starving of Khartoum,
quivering before the rain: the steel
thrust through the bowels, the mace
against the brain.

O Khartoum! Folly and Khartoum!

Someone rattled the door—or
was it the wind?

Slowly Gordon turned,
took up the book where he
had put his sister's name, *Augusta*.
He closed the book. Nothing would be pure,
neither east nor west,
nothing but man's folly,
and the breaking bones.

So inviolate in the sun, the she-goat moved
her legs, birth-heavy, mired in effort.
She was a quart of ground, dun,
the tips of her nose and ears
like pebbles, her udders
spots of gravel tinted by the sun.

When would they come? The enemy?
Lord Kitchener's army?

She had reached the crest, her
flank revealed, her head towards
the blue-green water of the river.

Gordon braced his hands against the ledge.
A distant bubble moved, a wedge
of shadow stirred by the wind
fell through the yard. A flash.
A flick of dull orange heat.
A dust of plaster fell across the view,
then cleared. The goat, fecund, carrying sin,
crumpled like paper in the wind.

The Arabs were moving now.

LOVE ON THE FRONTIER

How can I, she asked
of the man who had misled her,
promising what he saw
but had not really seen,
a skittering of ants.
How can I re-chink this cabin
when the snow everywhere
is over twelve feet deep?

She slapped his face.
He cringed then wept
and swept away her blows.
He was American. She was not.
She was loquacious, he was not.
She'd over-greased her black plaits.
The sun-sores on his cheeks
were salmon-red.
He had, it's true, produced a hare
seized with his own hands
during his descent.
He'd meant to bring a sack of gold
from high mountain streams
where in the depths
sun dispelled the chill
and water never froze.
Nothing worked.
He could not eschew whoring.
At least a fire blazed.
She'd chopped the wood.
Bleak flour sacks hung from a rope
deflecting heat within her well of comfort.

She calmed.
He sat on a stool

near the swollen iron stove
and warmed his feet.
He placed his old felt hat,
his stinking shirt and
woolen pants atop the stove.
They blazed.
When she tried to stem his wrath,
her blouse caught fire,
then her hair.
Appearing as a holy figure
in a husk, she clasped him,
pressing his back
against the burning metal.
Everything, all, would soon be ash.
Then, overgrowth of blueberry shrubs
would entice bears, bees,
wild fern, hazelnuts, cecropia, fireflies.

PREMONITION

I'll return again, said the face.
Oh no, replied the ear
and turned aside.
A finger stood erect, a shadow
rabbit's ear garnering messages
from the wind. The hand's palm
was red and wet.

There is pulp on the sidewalk.
By the water-fountain bird bath
a wren's heart is impaled on a thorn.

Love is gentler than sight.
That is its burden.

GAUGUIN'S CHAIR

The night is a lizard beneath my shirt.
The gas light is cold.
The candle I burn for you melts.
I would never whip a woman
nor trip a beggar
crawling in spittle in the street.
I intend to pay the rent.
Most beds are narrow.
A tree of lemons swung over ours.
Branches shook down black fat cherries.

I suck ribs and crack knee joints,
find wine and water in dream,
fever, hallucination.
Polyps cover my tongue. An arrow
rides through my throat and lungs.
Come back! See how the night
burns flowers around the door,
trees in the window.

In the dark I said
"God is not living in the valley,
he is staying here with us."
You said: "God is a lily of the valley,
He is steel."

That was before the black house rat
hung its brother from your easel,
where I found it, dying.
See how you leave me!

When you came to Provence
I possessed one shoe,
no socks or soap, wore no underwear.
My tongue ached for honey,

a rope over a rafter.
I had smashed my clock,
had no books, painted flowers
and apple trees in blood
thinned with urine, thickened
with dung. Only sheep
in the orchard saw me,
and gigantic sunflowers
waving hordes of bees.
I hate my lard white skin!
You almost drive me
to divert the world's vomit
back into its own throat.
You are halves of spiked iron
closing in on me.

I set the candle on your chair,
two books: arms, back and seat
of chair. The candle burns free
of the tip. Hot wire
through knuckles, through cheek,
tongue, loin, hip, and ankle.
My arms seem free, act.
The action cools my brain.
I can almost sing.

Outside, wheat fields swirl hair.
Seductive black birds—shock
patterns, brittle, raging, green.

I love you. I love you.
And if I had killed you
as you were dying I would have
held you, would have lain
full-length upon you
until
your feet were still.

V: PERSONAE

THE GIFT TO BE SIMPLE: MOTHER ANN LEE, FOUNDER OF THE SHAKERS

The mystic Ann Lee was born in Manchester, England in 1736. Her early visions convinced her followers that she was the Female Christ. After much persecution, accompanied by eight Believers, she sailed for America, settling near Albany, New York. She died at age forty-eight as the result of beatings she endured at the hands of mobs. Her faith led to the establishment of nineteen Shaker communities in America with over 5,500 members.

Gin and the King's Men

Gin and the king's men
again. The king's men again
and gin. The gin-soused woman
down the lane, the men near John
Lee's blacksmith shop again, and
gin, and the king's men begin.
Ann Lee in a chestnut tree,
aged ten: the gin-soused woman
and the king's men. The king's
men strip the gin-soused woman
and, again, she dances, her fat
tubs of butter in the wind.
The king's men throw her down, begin.
The woman, the gin, the king's men.

A Is For Ann: A Garland of Shaker ABC's

A is for *Apse* and *Altar* and *Aisle*, as A is for
  Ant, Angel, Apple, and *Ann.*

B is for *Benedict* the name of our cat, and B
  is for *Bangles* (worn especially by angels)

and B is for *Bed*, *Behemoth*, and *Bat*.

C is for *Chores* that we do in the house
   and C is for *Clutter* and *Cobwebs* and *Cathay*
   and C is for *Coffin* and *Codfish* and *Cherries*
   and C is for *Cloak* as well as for *Caries*.

D is for *Diamonds* and jewels in the skies, and
   D is for *Damask*, the trapping of Heaven,
   and D is the *Dawn* for pleasing our eyes.

E is for *Eggs* (hen, thrush, and duck), and
   E is for *Eels* wriggling in muck,
   and E is for *Evil* counting his losses,
   and E is for *Elephant* wreathing his proboscis.

F is for bull*Frog* and *Female* and *Fool*, and F
   is for *Fairies* dancing on a pool when
   marsh*Fires* are *Flaming*; and last but not least
   F is for *Forge* and *Father* and *Fleece*.

G is for *Grouse*, the poacher's delight, and G is for *Grace*
   to be said at each meal, and for *Goose* and *Gravy* and
   Gravestone and *Grunt*.

H is for *Holly* and *Holy* and *Hands* twined in prayer, and
   H is for *Hawthorne* bush, *Health*, and angel *Hair*.

I is for *Idols*, those we deplore, their names kept
   by the prophets in God's holy score; and I is
   for *Ice* that freezes our nose
   whenever *Injurious* cold winds blow.

J is for *Jay*, *Jesus*, *Jacob*, and *Jump*.

K is for *Kitten* asleep in the *Kitchen*, and for

Kestrel aloft soaring over the *Kirk*.

L is for *Lion* with bees in his belly, and L is for
Lion—fierce image of the *Lord*, and L is for
Lion—protector of the lamb.

M is for *Mother*, *Magpie*, and *Mad*, and for *Murder*
and *Mastiff* and *Marmot* and *Maw*, and for
Milk in the pail from the *Mooing* cow.

N is for *Nutting*, which we do in the fall, and
N is for *Nightingale*, which we seldom see at all,
and N is for *Near*, which the Lord is to thee.

O is for *Oven* where we bake our sweet bread, and O
is for *Over*, as in the cow and the mOOn, and O
is for *Open*, as our souls must be soon, and O
is for *Oak* and *Oat* and *Oar*, and O is *Obey* the
whirlwind's roar.

P is for *Parson* who looks like a *Parrot*
when he *Preaches* damnation in the *Pulpit*
on Sunday.

Q is for *Quince* and *Question* and *Quart*, and for
Quarries for marble, and limestone, and *Quartz*.

R is for *Rook* in the graveyard so mournful, and R is
for *Robins* and *Roses* and *Ruffians* and *Rout*.

S is for *Spinning* and *Sewing* fine *Seams*, and for
Smithy and *Soldier* and *Swine* and for *Steam*.
So, *Sit* here beside me, let's *Sing* a *Sweet Song*,
for our lives are so *Short* and Eternity long.

T is for *Thrift* which we practice each hour, and
T is for *Tidy* (so godlike and good), and T

is for *Titmouse* and *Thimble* and *Throat*.

U is for *Unity*, for God, Ghost, and Son, and U
  is for *Unicorn* that single-horned one. And U
    is for *Unwell*, which is mother's state: she coughs
  up blood at a frightening rate.

V is for *Violet*, and V is for *Vat*
  where we make soap with lye, ashes, and fat; and
    V is for *Vesper* that bright evening star, and
  V is for *Venus* the lover of Mars.

W is for *Wilderness*, *Wisdom*, and *Wit*;
  and W is for *Weaving* and *Wayward* and *Wax*
    for the *Web* of the spider, the *Wave* on the sea
  and the *Wattle* on the cock.

X, as always, is for *Xerxes* the King. Try, if you can
  to find some other thing.

Y is for *Yearling* dropped in the spring, and Y is for
  Yellow, *Yokel*, and *Yert*; and Y is for *Your* heart and
  Your soul and Y O U.

Z is for *Zeal*, *Zinc*, *Zero*, and *Zany*.
  And if you don't like Ann's alphabet, now that it's down
    she'll call old *Zymurgy* up from his cave to whirl you
      around.

Abraham Stanley

My husband doesn't intend the pain.
Carnality is an incredible thwarting
of the spirit, of *my* spirit.

I hardly allow myself to feel
tingling in my fingers without shame.
I avoid my reflections in water, pewter,
or tin. The mind subdues, translates
the body's aches into the blaze of God.

My gentle husband: his supple body
has the fragrance of oaks and maples.
It savors of forest ponds. His hairs
cling to his body. His back and thighs
are smooth pewter. I like the brush
and feel of his hair. But when I see
his gaze color with lust and see
his throat pulse, I pray
for our guardian angel to save us.

He strokes my hair.
I can't dissuade him.
His hands close over my breasts.
(I won't allow it. My breath is in a well.
My bones are wet, nay, in the wet well of death.)
I want to sing to God: Spirit, enter,
fasten our souls!

Abraham goes to the barn attached to the house.
The cow and the sheep are fed and safe.
The hens are safe. I go to bed, bundle in, in
prayer, a life in my womb, the first, a dear one,
Abraham's, conceived in sin. Let it be, I pray,
a girl, a gentle female for the work of the Lord,
in this world.

The bed shakes as he doffs his clothes.
He climbs in. I feel his hair. His member
pushes against my thighs. I whimper.
He raises my gown. Muscles along my legs

tighten and burn, my buttocks are taut,
my toes cramp. He pries me apart. "Be quick,"
I plead. "Be quick." I stifle moans in the pillow.
I am dry. The hurt! The hurt!
He strokes my neck, bites as he pumps to a pitch.
As he falls, there is a luminous angel: his feet
are curly and he blows a horn. His hair is silver,
his wings are rainbow-stained.
He loves me! He loves me! My angel loves me!

Elegy

Dead children's faces. Dead children
lying naked in the snow.
I walk up to them. Yes, I touch John.
He flees. I touch the others. They also
flee. I cannot succor them, they
cannot succor me. My spirit bleeds.
I see the imprints of their bodies in the snow.
The ice flows fast. Green grass struck with
miniature white flowers sprout where each child
has been. I kneel to kiss each spot, but my lips
press ice. I don't know where to go!
I stand and, moaning, pace that ground
until my husband hears my sound.
He strikes my face to stop the fit.
He leads me in, warms me, and helps me go to bed.

Feathers

Feathers have fallen from the sky before.
A bird knows that in light's careful and harsh
ambience his feathers fall. Mite-and-lice-tired

wings pluck loose, or breast feathers wrenched
by the wind loosen, painless, float as shadows
to a path, a lake, a pool. Each lost feather,
each quill, is puffed aside, when we find them,
smaller, lost over in silence.

Turning Song

Whatever is taken returns.
Whatever is lost is found.
Turn, turn, Believer, turn right round.

The sky again is blue.
The trapped hare is sprung.
Turn, turn, Believer, turn right round.

Whatever dies quickens.
Whatever is tied is unbound.
Turn, Turn, Believer, turn right round.

Whatever is eyeless, sees.
Whatever is dumb cries angel-sounds.
Turn, Believer, turn right round.

LUDWIG OF BAVARIA:
THE PICNIC IN THE SNOW

Ludwig II of Bavaria, 1845-1886, considered by some historians to be the last absolute European monarch, was a driven and tragic figure best remembered for his lavish patronage of Richard Wagner, for his building of the great castles at Neuschwanstein, Herrenchiemsee, and Linderhof, and for the mysterious circumstances surrounding his death, ostensibly by drowning, the day after he was deposed by Bavarian politicians. Known as "The Dream King," Ludwig spent much of the wealth of Bavaria on the pursuit of Beauty and Art, eschewing war and politics for the sake of his dreams and visions. His struggle over his homosexuality was yet another tension in his vivid life.

Royal Swan

A swan's magnificent trachea
coils within its sternum.
Aroused, it sounds a canticle
blown through the twists
and brass turns of a trumpet.
A swan carols when it dies.
Swan-throats carol the deaths of kings
and princes. My own blood's salt
is swan-salt. My palms taste of feathers.
I ruffle the surfaces of lakes.

Horses

A horse can rarely vomit, or belch gas.
The stomach does not absorb, and the outlet
by the bowels is one hundred feet long.
This organ is often ruptured, with fatal results.
A horse with acute distention lowers its head

to the ground. It sweats profusely, lies
on the sternum with the front feet extended
and raises the body. The mucous membranes
of the eye are scarlet.
Twisted and distorted hooves,
bruises of the sole, ringbone,
ossified cartilage, sprains
of the flexor tendon, diseases
of the fetlock, postern and coffin joints.
Corns, bruises, pricks, quottors,
sandcracks, thrush, canker, sidebone,
laminitis, navicular disease, contracted hoof,
loose wall, hollow wall and graveling.
During each coitus guard against dourine,
glanders, genital eczema, horse pox,
mange, and contagious abortion.
Following a twist of the bowel
an onset of colitis is sudden, marked
by continuous pain. A rotation of the intestine
cuts off all circulation. There is no cure.

Horses like to run, and men pursue them.

Richard Wagner at the Keyboard

Your fingers on the keyboard.
Your head bowed intent on a cadenza.
Outside the window,
afternoon snow, late, tumultuous.

We have been here over six hours:
the velvet drapes, the peacock, the fern,
the fire, the rosewood of the piano
intensified by the flames.

Each note you score, each chord
thrust past its fumbling, sutures
the world, healing what was rent,
is once again made whole.

I am vexed, though, Wagner, *Seele*,
that as you create and I observe—yes, yes,
inspiring you, I can't see your splendid hands
as Apollo must, or the years
clanging down immense corridors.

Alas, my eyes are jellies.
My ears thrum from being too near
flamboyant trumpet voluntaries.
I can't hear your sounds as you do!
I have banished all trumpets from the Court!

The Gray Goose

A gray goose with a dulcimer, playing
for its dinner, hoped to find its liver
which it dropped in a meadow. A poacher
came upon it, dazzled by the aroma
and the deepening shade of purple.
The flies, too, rampant, nibbled off
choice pieces, until frightened by a chicken
who squawked and dropped her liver
in that same spot by the river.
The poacher then decided that livers are generic
and while reaching for the goose's
his own thick organ loosened
and tumbled to the ground.

Richard Hornig

1.

Unpack the wine, Hornig. Spread a cloth on the snow
there, near that spruce with the pitch-green branches.
Portion the roast quail, the brisket, the potatoes,
the mousse. Later serve the brandied coffee.
A proximity to ice improves your appetite,
so why are you shivering? The sun is beneficent.
Note the warmly-colored unicorns
prancing on the tablecloth among the roses.
They aren't cold, why are you?
Stop shivering! I command you!
Scoop out a snowdrift for your velvet cushion.
Pretend we're sheik and loyal retainer
picnicking on the sand at Samarcand.

2.

If, Hornig, as you say, your body craves mine,
I shall believe you, though I know you fantasize.
Henceforth you shall own a house, a dray horse,
a carriage, and shall sail along behind me, at
my speed. Seeing you this evening, my lips
tremble at the fusion: the torsion of my ugliness,
your pulchritude. You are a creature foaled
in the moon's house. You are the scrotum of God
made flesh!

Love

Love is a motion in the loins, or, so I've assumed.
Love's pinions drag and flap in the missionary position.
In love's mansion there is but one room.
Eros perfumes his genitals with civet every afternoon.
I am waiting, Endymion, to waft you to the moon.
Love wipes his fundament on the neck of a loon.
Flatulence and pyorrhea, headaches and diarrhea!
A flabby paunch and a flabby ass
had best be jellied and kept under glass
or combined with goose liver into a pâté
and served with mint sauce on Christmas Day.

The People

I won't bow and smile at those people!
I won't be stared at!
I won't come out of my shell, as you say it!
I will not attend the festivities for my family,
the seven hundredth anniversary of the Wittelsbachs!
Herr Secretary, I am staying where you will not find me.
I'm a wasp outside a stable in love with bedrooms.
I wish I were a dahlia, or a white marguerite
plucked on an amazing night of gauze and tulle.
I wish I were a mushroom, phallus of the mountain,
burgeoned through the mulch after hours of tempest,
then grazed and shattered by a stag's hoof.

How else may I numb my aches? My inflamed gums!
The ball bone of my hip grinds glass.
I'm a wasp outside a stable in love with bedrooms.
My gender's wrong!
If I could find that wretched vesicle,
I'd rip it forth and cast it to the weasels!

Ludwig Invites His Favorite Horse
Cosa Rara To Dinner

Calm him, groom. What are you doing with that white
tablecloth? Don't tie it around his neck.
He's a horse. He's not human. That's why I need him.
Bring the candles closer. Fine. Now depart.

Cosa Rara, your gilt tray, my priceless china.
If only Herr Wagner were here to dine with us.
At this moment his "Siegfried" is being performed in Venice.

Eat, Cosa Rara, eat. Your oats were steeped in cognac
and toasted. Heaps of Alpine clover powdered,
even glazed with sugar. Wheat-kernels plumped in Moselle.

Alas, I am not hungry. My robe stifles me.
My stomach sags over my belt.
Horse, your eyes are as wild as mine.
They mock the insipidity of the world.
Let the politicians, the generals, and the painted dowagers waffle and
bob until they sink!
Send them off to the stables without their wigs and dinners!

Cosa Rara! Don't leave! Stay the night! *Stay* the night!

THE BLOOD COUNTESS:
ERZEBET BATHORY OF HUNGARY

Erzébet Bathory (1560-1614) believed she would remain young by bathing in the blood of virgins. She slaughtered some 700 women before she was immured in her castle, in 1611. She devised exquisite tortures, and was not to be outdone by her famous ancestor Vlad the Impaler. Her fascination with furs, jewels, and fine music intensified her brutality. She anticipates today's numerous serial killers. She even gloats over the fact that our times, sicker than hers, have made this aberration our very own.

I live under the pearl.
My gorget is pearl encrusted.
My gloves at the finger joints
stiffen with pearls.
My chestnut tresses, bleached blonde
by rinsing in the potent ocher
of saffron, washed by retainers,
are dried before huge flaming candles
then gathered up in a snood of pearls.
My nerves coil through savage mists.
I swallow pearls.

* * *

The moon's in Capricorn.
I bathe in bitter resin.
Later, rubbed dry, in my crypt,
I draw pentagrams, evoking vulpine powers.
A girl stands near, and I bite her.

O vulva. O moon-rind breasts.
O patella smeared with hemoglobin compote.
O powdered opals swirled in hot Burgundy.
O diphthongs of lust spurting...

* * *

Be warned. I shall keep nothing from you.
We are at the castle dairy.
Smell the delicious hay and the fragrant cow udders.
I am wearing my red kazabaika.
I dress appropriately for all occasions.
My dwarf Dobrin is joining me.

Dobrin, where have you been?
Gushes of menstrual blood soak my sheepskin.
And why are those mangers empty?
My cows must never want for the juiciest
grasses and clovers.

In that stanchion is my favorite cow,
the red one, garlanded,
with the swollen udder and the magnificent teats.

With Dobrin's help, I shove a bench under the cow.
I lie there with my knees up, my legs apart.
I caress the plump udder, find the largest
and hardest of the teats.
I insert it slowly.
Gushes of hot milk!
"Lick me clean, Dobrin. Lick me clean."

Never trust your servants. Self-abuse is always best.

* * *

I will kick, lacerate, bite,
bruise, impale and macerate
their bodies, but never
those Venusian parts
ridged like peach pits sodden

bubbling when aroused.

* * *

Plum and rose water
traced down the labia.
a shiver as if a whisker bristled.

* * *

Roast leg of lamb
resembles roast leg of man.
Sausage, stuffed with hogs,
humans or dogs.
Hemoglobin mousse
of Transylvanian peasant!
Bathory flambé!

I bit an apple and a neighbor.
She was a dull girl
a mushroom gatherer.
I pricked my thumb on a needle.
Nurse crossed herself, wheedled
and swore to the Virgin.
My bloody pinafore!
I sucked with a crazy fervor.
Oily, yes, a rare nectar.

* * *

Jesus, after dining, horrors may occur.
I prefer my communion wafers plain
marinated in Your blood.
Jesus, my virgins are images of Your mother.
I've secured their purity forever
in homage to You, Lord.

Was the pain of the murderer on Golgotha
less than yours?
Jesus, God Your Father is the primal mass murderer.
Everything dies. That's His plan.

God! You are required to kill more creatures
than You alone are able to kill.
Is madness my birthright, bestowed by You?
Not for nothing do I come from a long line
of kings, bishops, and abbots.
I am one of your Avenging Angels!
That's why I was born!

Jesus bleeds. I bleed.
My blood, alas, is human.

* * *

Stop, near that freezing pond.
Wipe the blood from my face.
I had not intended to bite her so viciously.
Now, hot wine in that silver goblet
depicting the nymphs bathing.

How beautifully the pond steams.
By evening it will be frozen solid.

Remove her clothes and slippers!
Kick her from the carriage!
Tie her to that spruce near the freezing pond.

Girl, you'll never remember this.
You'll numb slowly as you turn to ice.
Drench her with pond water! Drench her!

She's visible now as a shimmer!
A chess piece of ice!

My cabriolet roof is burning!
I create this weather!

* * *

Another Christmas.

Dear children! Kató, fetch me my jewels. You seem much better this season. The coughing and the headaches have subsided. Orsik, you startled me when you said you wished to be King of Poland. Your father is sending you your very own dwarf, and you shall have that Christmas pudding crammed with oranges, persimmons, apples, and dates. Anna, precious, you shall have a gown trimmed in silver with puffed red velvet sleeves and a neck-ruff as stiff and lovely as one of my very best. You have been such good children. How I love you all! I will sing for you a carol my nurses sang to me when I was a child: "Good King Wenceslaus looked out / on the feast of Stephen..."

* * *

Dear Husband, though I sound cheerful
I am frightened. Maelstroms, seizures.
Neither Palestrina nor Gesualdo relieve the symptoms.
My tears are hot stones.

Beloved Ferencz, won't prolonged prayers
coat your tongue and invite exotic diseases?
Do keep muffled. Take all the mistresses you need.

You are standing outside my door eating oranges.
You are wearing embroidered slippers and a velvet
cod piece. You throw a gold net mesh over me.
I shall order the altar flagstones warmed.
Wine in goblets of lapis lazuli
anastomosed with grains of powdered gold.
Then I shall kiss your eyes and listen,
as a good wife should.
I have been a good wife, haven't I?

ELISHA KENT KANE:
AMERICAN ARCTIC EXPLORER

Kane (1820-1857) was an indefatigable American hero who, afflicted with rheumatic fever, led two expeditions to the Arctic searching for the English explorer Sir John Franklin. This book is based on the journals and letters Kane kept during his second ill-fated voyage, in 1854, when his brig froze fast in the ice off the east coast of Greenland. It's apparently still there. Kane not only served as commander but also as physician, research scientist, and record keeper.

Sea-Fire

Pancreatic, visceral
pink, orange, and blue—
tones of mesoderm, as the scalpel
slivers fat: lung-hues, pink suet
slogged all over the heart and bowels:
the ocean so cold
the foot-webs of gulls freeze
touching it, so alive
it crests and throbs choking, delirious,
with ice-fever.

Eatables

At very low temperatures
our eatables laughably consolidate:
dried apples are a brachiated mass
of impacted angularities,
a conglomerate of sliced chalcedony.
The best plan is to chop both fruit and barrel,
later thawing the lumps.
Sauerkraut resembles mica
or rather talcose slate.

A crowbar extracts the laminae badly.
Nothing but the saw suits our sugar.
Butter and lard
require a cold chisel and mallet.
Their fracture is conchoidal,
with an hematic (iron-ore pimpled) surface.
Pork and beef are specimens of Florentine
mosaic, emulating the lost art of
petrified, visceral monstrosities
treasured under glass
at the medical schools of Milan and Bologna.

On Capturing Ducks

A bolsa is a swift device
for dropping ducks to the ice:
tie ivory weights to braided sinew
and as the ducks come winging past you
let your multiple gadget fly
flipping upwards towards the sky.
With luck the weights will snag a duck
and choke its neck and break its back.

The human voice is fine in fog
for dropping eiders on the bog:
their feathers are so stiff and soaked
their clumsy bodies sailing low
can't veer and swing and bank for danger.
Hide yourself in their line of flight
and shout aloud with all your might.
Slogged with wet, they try to turn
but freezing, frenzied, drop and churn
amidst the snow, frantic to elude your blow.
You wring their necks with a practiced flip

then quickly grab and whirl your bolsa
as more sodden ducks wing towards you.

Dr. Kane With His Etah Hosts

1.

Kolopsuts smoke
with a burden of seal-flippers.
Each matron's *kotluk* flames.
The Etah use their soup pots
for boiling stew and urinating.
The nearest Eskimo word for *dirt*
is *Eberk*: it hardly suffices.

2.

The ammoniacal steam
of fourteen
unwashed, unclothed Eskimo
jammed into an igloo,
temperature ninety degrees,
all twined, covered in native suet,
juicy worms in a fishing basket.
I eat some frozen liver nuts,
perspire, then undress, like the rest
and cross Mrs. Eider's naked breasts,
pillow my head on Myouk's manly chest,
and, as an honored guest, enjoy a blissful rest.

Crippled Light-Rays, Fevers

Begin here today: snow needles the tent.
Vexed teeth rip the canvas. Heat waves drift
from my candle, meant to thaw my fingers
sorting these papers—crippled moth-wings,
gossamer shreds of what we so bravely spend,
crushed between hummocks of ice. My throat
won't clear itself. Crippled rays of light
blear what will be my (our) last testament—
should we freeze and these notes survive.
For, as we starve—fevered shapes are crouching,
and the men, sick with diarrhea and scurvy
must either stench themselves
or use that icy pan beneath the table—
I record how we have pushed further north
than any other men of our race. I record
our thirst for green leaves, citrus,
a female face. I record our hates.
an enormous spill empties my brain.
My heart's tubes clog with ice.
I won't suffer! I say "wait!"
I strike whale bone through my heart.

Rats

A rat bit my finger to the bone
last Friday. I was intruding my hand
into a bearskin mitten, one she had chosen
as a homestead for her family.

I have devised traps for the rats.
If we cannot kill them all
we'll reduce their numbers.

This morning, we catch six near the flour.
We dump them chattering
into a cylinder of chloroform.
I retrieve them, comatose,
and, carefully, with my scalpel
divest them of their pelts,
viscera, and extremities.
The rosy flesh I toss into a pot,
add salt and a few dried apples.
Though the result is tasty
I never eat the head, innards,
or the fat behind the eyes.

Starving Dogs

Alas, our supply of dogs is low,
as is our meat. They eat walrus
and are ravenous.
They whine, yip, and chase their tails.
Some must be shot.
The huskies eat their pups
but won't eat one another
unless we butcher them.

Today we found a bow-head whale
buried four years ago. We sliced
its tongue, some hundred pounds,
into felt-like pieces.
The dogs eat, and we eat too.

The meat, though we boil it four times,
is tough and salty. A quinine bitterness.
We boil eight bear paws and a deerskin.

We boil and eat shoe-lashings and rawhide
thongs. Cooked rawhide resembles pig's feet.
We are wretched.

These Things Are Gray

Arctic goose, gun metal,
rat, greylag, Franciscan,
grayback, whalebone, hooded-crow,
birch, dogfish, hound,
fox, griege, gray gum, butterflies,
manganese ore, brain matter,
squirrel, graywacke, grayling,
graywether, graypate—
the insidious tones
shrouding the Arctic for 140 days
commencing in mid-October.

Smallpox decimates the Eskimo.
Cairns of the victims, abandoned huts,
implements of the chase interlace
along the coast.

Noluk, the graceful hunter,
drives his sledge homeward
carrying meat for his wife.
He sees her through an igloo window.
His infant son, frozen, sucks
a frozen teat. Without entering,
Noluk makes his way South.

ROBERT HAWKER:
CORNISH VICAR, MYSTIC, AND POET

Hawker is based on the life of an eccentric vicar (1802-1875) who served an impoverished parish on the bleak, northern Cornish coast, an area overlooking a wild portion of the sea noted for shipwrecks. Hawker saw it as his special mission to rescue drowned sailors and give them proper burials. He also played mermaid for his parishioners. He was something of a Victorian St. Francis, loving animals for attending his church services. His eccentric dress included a claret cassock, yellow wool poncho, fisherman's sweater and boots, and a red hat. He is famous for having written the Cornish National Anthem.

Animals, Oh!

Nine cats have I this season, in church and out.
They regale the air with their mews,
rubbing my legs with their whiskers.
Let them lap up warm milk in the belfry
and squat in the vestry.

Old Cat though has sorely vexed me.
He ate a mouse in Church on Sunday, near the altar.
I excommunicate him. He leaves me grieving.

Among the gentlest of breathing creatures
is the cow. None shows
more passionate tenderness for its young
when deprived of them.
None shows more wonderfully striated colors
in its eyes than when it's busy at its cud.
None steps more gracefully, full-uddered,
through a slimy pond, barely nicking the lilies.
And when it's beaten it hunches
its long backbone, shudders, and for protection
bunches together with other cows.

Animals are the visible attributes of God
roaming this earth.

Gyp, My Loving Big Black Pig: An Acrostic Poem

Gyp goes with me everywhere.
You'll find him in church on a Sunday
Pillowed upon clean straw, to the east of the altar.

Muffling his whiffles, reserving grunts of pleasure,
Yeasty eructations, for the noisier hymns and carols.

Lively and contented, wiggling his quirky tail
Over the coombes and valleys, he trots behind the
Vicar as he visits his parishioners—
In house, in cot, in glebe and pasture,
Never once despoiling a humble hearth-stone,
Glad to be sociable, he jiggles his globular testes.

Brushing a floppy ear means he wants a good scratching.
In storm, in sun, the elements ne'er dissuade him:
Gloriously he wallows in the finest muck-holes

Believing he's in Paradise, awash in tarry ichor.
Later I must scrub him and oil his hide with suet.

After that we'll take our tea with good Dorothy Dinglett.
Coarse he is outside 'tis true, but within he's all refinement.
Know, ye cynics, and be warned: and model your own deportment

Pig-wise, Gyp-wise. You'll surely feel an improvement
In manners as well as morals. And when you next devour pork
Grant a special whiff of thanks to Black Gyp and his tribe.

Song

Devil's Ring, Dozmere Pool,
Dragon-crest of a Viking.

Kilmarth Tor and the Rowter,
Hail the Mort d'Arthur.

Cartha Martha, Tamar Spring
Celtic barbarians.

Hennacliff and Raven's Crag
King Ethelwolf and Edith.

Morwenstowe, and dear Morwenna
Patron Saint of Cornwall.

On Trying To Reach A Ship In Distress

1.

The tide drives us baffled from the spot
before we grasp the ship's mast.
Rifted stones rise and hurl
along the shuddering marge.
The ship lies in smithereens.

2.

The bloated bodies of a mate and three men.
None has the placid mien
of those drowned by accident,
or of those dead in their beds.
The officer's countenance is grim.

Was he driven from his deck
by a crew despising him?

3.

Most sailors have arms pricked with tracery—
initials, wreaths, anchors, and forget-me-nots.
I record such marks in the church-log.
Such pictures, these poor dear men assumed,
would illume their identities.
What resignation! to wear on your living flesh,
as if it were for forever, your sepulchral name.

Churchwarden: "Why, Sir, when we used to find dead sailors on the
shore, and carried them in, you didn't so give way, as you do now,
weeping when you go into the Church."

Hawker: "Spare me the misery and, indeed, the proximity, to those
advanced in decay! A debasing terror. A dying sailor. A driven leaf
frightens me helter-skelter. Tick-tick. Death-Day. Mine.

Black John

How strange you are, you humped,
elfin-haired provocateur of mice and sparrows.

The lilac blossom
and the thistle, master,
burnish the rose.

In your loose, black, flabby mouth
your teeth have long since ceased to harmonize.

Go faster sparrow or he'll nab you.
Scurry, mouseling to your wainscot corner.

How many shillings did you earn
for "mumbling" birds and swallowing mice?
You slept curled, in all weather, under hedgerows.

Tie a sparrow to a string
attached to a tooth.
"Mumble" off all feathers
by mouth alone, including
those encircling the fundament,
until the bird shivers, bare.
Secure a mouse-leg by a cord,
then swallow the creature.
Its toes scratch your throat.
Its fur induces coughing.
When we shout you yank it forth
saliva-drenched and puling.
You spew rage.
I mean your good, Black John.

Cancer

I cannot face misery.
I am too much the eudaemonist.
I miss my wife Charlotte greatly.
Grief wells in my digits and my body.
My heart is livid stone.
The tendrils rushing my blood hither
scald. Cancer flames through my viscera.
Pistils and stamens shiver with pain.
Opium dissolves the gloomy umbrage of my mind.
Tentaculae of cancer wither away.

Opium Haze Christmas Poem

My terrified wife is by my bed.
Her hands drip wax.
Her eye-holes are bleached purple,
a noumenal shade.
I drift, to the clang of cutlery
banging on metal, to the clack of teeth
in an iron kettle.

Brawny legs in violet gaiters
float near the ceiling.
A drowned sailor's breast.
Skeletal hands grasp for others
lurking in a beam.
A stubbled tongue protrudes
from a swirl of ivy in a glass.

I hear everything: the cat's saliva drool,
the furry spider on my cheek, the plop
of an egg from a hen, a sand-sift of voices
mellifluous, like pulled-taffy
in the hands of my mother at Yuletide.

My children, in sun-stroke, crowd round my bed.
I see their Christmas shoes, their worsted
stockings, their frocks, their gay ribbons.
I take each satiny child-face and kiss and kiss,
until my dear wife draws the darlings from me
fearing I will bruise them.
I am so drugged!

BENJAMIN ROBERT HAYDON: VICTORIAN PAINTER

Haydon (1776-1846) studied under the Swiss painter Fuseli, and was a friend of Keats, Wordsworth, Hazlitt, Lamb, the Carlyles, and the Brownings. Because of a difficult, non-compromising temperament, he was ignored by the Royal Academy, and so found himself and his large family in great distress. He insisted on painting vast history pictures in the grand style, a mode much out of favor with the Victorian public. He was imprisoned for debt many times, and decided that only by suicide could he feed his family: there would be a public subscription of monies. He botched the job, using a pistol with too small a bore to penetrate his skull, and only by resorting to a straight razor did he manage to kill himself. Money was collected to support his family.

Haydon Sketches the Elgin Marbles and Wrestles With His Art

Woke up intending to reform my person,
not the vanity-ridden husk
of the flat-bellied man I am
whose neck cloths are stained
no matter how much I scrub and
rub in jasmine. I'll not eat
a single cake this entire day.

The greatest blessing brought to this country
ever are the Elgin Marbles.
By sketching in the missing limbs
of Theseus and Ilyssus
I seed my brain's landscape.

Half past four, dawn, a ghastly hour
yet one conducive to preliminaries:
a quick sketch of a mare's skull, a cat's femur.
I am not a bungler. I feel "right" towards the marbles.

I sketch a Centaur's back, a vulgar
porter-like form of a burdened man.
I'm slow, a signal always of a bloated brain.
A passing cloud sickens the skylight.
Should my Dentatus wear a heeled sandal?
Should the ligatures of a torso appear
in upright figures as they appear on the
backside of a bent torso?
I have just turned thirty-four.

Defeated, weeping, I rub out the chest
of my dying figure. Rising, I jar
a Lapith haunch which falls from its pedestal
cutting my leg. Much blood. It screamed
when it fell.

You must forgive me, bow to the east,
stroke your cat's throat, then
stroke yourself (or your mistress)
and think of me behind the butcher's
shop of time (eighteen o nine).

Mot

A tomb is a good place for a harem
for women should have something important to look at.

John Keats Sits For Haydon

Keats is of middle-size, with a low forehead,
eyes with the inward look of a Delphian priestess.
"Fix your eye on the horizon, Haydon."
He hopes to discover the "human dusthole"
where his dead brother lies.
His voice is feminine. Shelley's is masculine.

Keats falls ill and shortly dies.
I see him for the last time in his bed.
He had few hopes, stretched on life's horrid wrack.
To intensify his appetite, he peppered his tongue
the better to savor cold claret.
He appears in my *Christ Entering Jerusalem*
with Wordsworth, Lamb, and Hazlitt.

Sick Children

A new day slips forth.
A moth feeds on spittle,
traversing my lip, cheek, and startled eye.
It sips water from my lid
then treks to my forehead.
My brain swelters.
A voice of dinner pans.
Spine-chilling rattling of femurs and tibias.
A tinted meadow, a cloissoné stream.
Clappers tinkling inside lilies.

Two, no three, children, their feet
tangled in bluebells. "Papa! Papa!"
They're dead!
Their finger bones interlace, their skulls
have shreds of hair, their jaws are agape.
Hummingbirds of blood well from their throats!
I'll not be tricked again!
I'll hasten to join them!

The End

The hottest, most airless summer on record,
"a sultry month." I burn letters and papers,
pack my valuables to be sold:
the drawings of Wellington, Wordsworth, Keats,
and of my wife and dead children, and my journals.
I carry all to Elizabeth Barrett
who'll keep them from my creditors; she's promised.

Miss Barrett, in purple, reclines on a sofa.
(The evening is stifling.)
Flush sleeps in her lap.
She strokes him as she is speaking.
I'm lost in a wish to sketch her,
and rehearse the thin lines of her mouth,
the cheek bones, the tendrils scooping her temples.

"I want to die," I exclaim.

Monday, June 22, 1846.

I stop at Riviere, the gun maker, in Oxford Street.
Purchase small pistols.
At 9, I breakfast alone, then go to my painting-room.
As usual, I lock myself in.
I write letters to my children,
rewrite my will, and sketch final thoughts.
My daughter Mary, my confidante,
suspects nothing when she tries the door.
She says (through the door) that she and her mother
are going out. "Very well," I say.
Impulsively, I go to her, kiss her, and linger.
Though there is much to say, I walk away.

I load the pistol, poise a lone straight razor near.
It's 10:45. I face the door.
Noise in the street.
The hot air is a pall.
I squeeze the trigger.
Its small caliber deflects along the bone.
Why, even now, in this must I fail!
Desperate, I grab the open razor
and slice my throat from ear to ear!

Finis. Benjamin Robert Haydon.

A SELECTED BIBLIOGRAPHY

SELECTED PUBLICATIONS, INTERVIEWS, ETC.

An * indicates that the book is now out of print. Copies of most may be ordered directly from the author at 9431 Krepp Drive, Huntington Beach, CA 92646.

POEMS

SONGS FOR A SON, W. W. Norton, 1967.
THE SOW'S HEAD AND OTHER POEMS, Wayne State U. P., 1968.
*CONNECTIONS: IN THE ENGLISH LAKE DISTRICT, Anvil Press (London), 1972
*RED MIDNIGHT MOON, Empty Elevator Shaft, 1973.
*HOLY COW: PARABLE POEMS, Red Hill, 1974.
*BRONCHIAL TANGLE, HEART SYSTEM, Granite Books, 1975.
*COOL ZEBRAS OF LIGHT, Christopher's Books, 1975.
THE GIFT TO BE SIMPLE: A GARLAND FOR ANN LEE, Liveright, 1975.
*THE POET AS ICE SKATER, Manroot Books, 1976.
*GAUGUIN'S CHAIR: SELECTED POEMS 1967-1974, Crossing Press, 1977.
*HAWTHORNE, Red Hill, 1977.
THE DROWNED MAN TO THE FISH, New Rivers, 1978.
*IKAGNAK: THE NORTH WIND, Kenmore Press, 1978.
*CELEBRITIES: IN MEMORY OF MARGARET DUMONT, Sombre Reptiles, 1981.
*THE PICNIC IN THE SNOW: LUDWIG OF BAVARIA, New Rivers, 1982.
*WHAT DILLINGER MEANT TO ME, Sea Horse Press, 1983.
LOVE POEMS FOR ROBERT MITCHUM, privately printed, 1983.
*HAWKER, Unicorn Press, 1984.
*KANE, Unicorn Press, 1985.
*SHAKER LIGHT, Unicorn Press, 1986.
*LUDWIG OF BAVARIA: POEMS AND A PLAY, Cherry Valley, 1986.
*THE BLOOD COUNTESS: POEMS AND A PLAY, Cherry Valley, 1987.
*HAYDON, Unicorn Press, 1988.
*BRUEGHEL'S PIG, Illuminati, 1990.
GOOD NIGHT, PAUL, GLB Publishers, 1992.

CRITICISM, SCHOLARSHIP, MISCELLANEOUS

*VICTORIANS ON LITERATURE AND ART, Appleton Century, 1961.
*AMERICA: THE DIARY OF A VISIT, BY EDMUND GOSSE, Purdue U. P., 1966

*THE LETTERS OF JOHN ADDINGTON SYMONDS, ed. with H. Schueller, 3 vols., Wayne State U. P., 1967-1969.
*PIONEERS OF MODERN POETRY, with George Hitchcock, Kayak Press, 1967.
THE GREAT AMERICAN POETRY BAKE-OFF, 4 vols., Scarecrow Press, 1979, 1983, 1986, 1991.
THE PETERS BLACK AND BLUE GUIDE TO LITERARY JOURNALS, 3 vols., Cherry Valley, Dustbooks, 1983, 1985, 1987.
LETTERS TO A TUTOR: THE TENNYSON FAMILY LETTERS TO HENRY GRAHAM DAKYNS, Scarecrow Press, 1989.
ROBERT PETERS VISITS WILLIAM S. BURROUGHS, privately printed, limited edition, 1991.
SNAPSHOTS FOR A SERIAL KILLER: A FICTION, GLB Publishers, 1992.

INTERVIEWS

With Billy Collins, in Gauguin's Chair: Selected Poems, Crossing Press, 1977.
With Richard Peabody, in Gargoyle Magazine: "Poet Robert Peters Exposes Himself" (Jan. 1981, 21-25), reprinted as "Burn the Movies! The Gargoyle Interview," in The Great American Poetry Bake-off: Second Series, Scarecrow Press, 1983, 306-319.
With William Matthews, "The Shaker Poems," in The Great American Poetry Bake-off: Second Series, Ibid., 141-150.
With Don Mark, in Gay Sunshine Interviews II, Gay Sunshine Press, 1982, 123-141.
With Penelope Moffett, "Life on the Outside: Robert Peters," in Electrum, 1985, 32-35.
With Philip K. Jason, in The Signal, Oct. 1987, 17-23. Also in The Great American Poetry Bake-off: Fourth Series, 1991.
With Paul Trachtenberg, in Paintbrush, Autumn 1987, 43-49; also in The Great American Poetry Bake-off: Fourth Series, 1991.
Featured in the Writers' Autobiography Series, Vol. VIII, Gale Research Co., Dec. 1989.

ESSAYS ON ROBERT PETERS

Diane Wakoski, in American Poetry, Winter 1985, 71-78.
Diane Wakoski, in Connecticut Poetry Review, 1987, 11-18.
Edward Butscher, "The Personae of Daily Lives," in Contact II, Winter 1987, 78-79.
Billy Collins, "Literary Reputation and the Thrown Voice," in A Gift of Tongues: Critical Challenges in Contemporary American Poetry, eds. Marie Harris and Kathleen Augero, University of Georgia Press, 1987, 295-306.
Charles Hood, "Robert Peters," for the Dictionary of Literary Biography. "Robert Peters," in The Great American Poetry Bake-off: Fourth Series, 1991.
Philip K. Jason, "Robert Peters: Guts and Gusto," in The Great American Poetry Bake-

off: Fourth Series, 1991.

Edward Butscher, "Robert Peters," in *The Great American Poetry Bake-off: Fourth Series*, 1991.

Todd Moore, "Naming the Archetypes: The Major Poetry of Robert Peters," in *The Great American Poetry Bake-off: Fourth Series*, 1991.

NOTE: All of Robert Peters's papers from 1950-1990, including letters, manuscripts (both published and unpublished), and journals containing his poetry and prose, are on deposit in the Spenser Special Collections Library, the University of Kansas, Lawrence. His working library of contemporary poetry, with related papers, is now in the Rare Book Collection, Bowling Green State University.

Peters has served as a Contributing Editor for *The American Book Review*, *Contact II*, and *Paintbrush*. He has also judged competitions for fellowships and prizes for an assortment of small presses and for the Poetry Society of America and PEN International. He has enjoyed Guggenheim and National Endowment for the Arts fellowships, and won the Alice de Castagnola Prize of the Poetry Society of America, the Larry P. Fine Prize for Criticism, and the Kerouac Award for Poetry.